I have known Steve Richard for (......... ..... of that time he and his wife have been members of my church. Over the years I have watched him develop in his walk with the Lord as a husband, a father of three, and a businessman. Steve has been offered ideal job opportunities in the past from people who seemed to have promised him the moon. I have stood in prayer with him as he has navigated his family through these opportunities, always giving God the final authority in his decisions. He never moved off his principles or the discipline he and his wife have in dealing with such things on a frequent basis. I have found Steve to be a man who lives what he believes.

A King's Journey is giving us a glimpse into how Steve lives his life. He is sharing the key truths that he has learned from the Word of God to direct him successfully through the challenges life throws at all of us. His cutting-edge analogies are relevant and help bring clarity to this generation that is in an otherwise unstable world.

—PASTOR THOMAS PEETZ
WORD OF LIFE CHRISTIAN FELLOWSHIP
CONCORD, NH

A KING'S JOURNEY

A HANDBOOK FOR FULFILLING THE CALL OF GOD ON YOUR LIFE

STEVE RICHARD

CREATION
HOUSE

A King's Journey by Steve Richard
Published by Creation House
A Charisma Media Company
600 Rinehart Road
Lake Mary, Florida 32746
www.charismamedia.com

Unless otherwise noted, all Scripture quotations are from the King James Version of the Bible.

Scripture quotations marked THE MESSAGE are from *The Message: The Bible in Contemporary English*, copyright © 1993, 1994, 1995, 1996, 2000, 2001, 2002. Used by permission of NavPress Publishing Group.

Scripture quotations marked NKJV are from the New King James Version of the Bible. Copyright © 1979, 1980, 1982 by Thomas Nelson, Inc., publishers. Used by permission.

Scripture quotations marked NLT are from the Holy Bible, New Living Translation, copyright © 2007. Used by permission of Tyndale House Publishers, Inc., Wheaton, IL 60189. All rights reserved.

Scripture quotations marked AMP are from the Amplified Bible. Old Testament copyright © 1965, 1987 by the Zondervan Corporation. The Amplified New Testament copyright © 1954, 1958, 1987 by the Lockman Foundation. Used by permission.

Design Director: Bill Johnson
Cover design by Terry Clifton
Interior images designed by Andrew Spencer

Visit the author's website: https://www.facebook.com/akingsjourney

Library of Congress Cataloging-in-Publication Data: 2013946755
International Standard Book Number: 978-1-62136-672-0 (paperback)
International Standard Book Number: 978-1-62136-671-3 (hardback)
E-book International Standard Book Number: 978-1-62136-673-7

While the author has made every effort to provide accurate telephone numbers and Internet addresses at the time of publication, neither the publisher nor the author assumes any responsibility for errors or for changes that occur after publication.

First edition

13 14 15 16 17 — 9 8 7 6 5 4 3 2 1
Printed in Canada

DEDICATION

I HAVE DEDICATED THIS book to my amazing wife, Michele, who has traveled this incredible adventure by my side. You have helped me in this journey called life more times than you will ever realize. You are the greatest gift the Lord has ever given me.

CONTENTS

INTRODUCTION

MANY YEARS AGO I started hearing about this topic in the Bible, of kings and priests. Although I did not realize at the time what the implication of this would mean in my life, I knew it was right, and I knew I needed to seek the Lord for more understanding. The only issue was, there was little written on the subject until more recently. Every time I would read about this topic of kings or talk about it with my wife, Michele, something would go off on the inside. Although the seed for understanding this truth of kings and priests was first planted in my heart in the early 2000s, this book is really a compilation of the things that God has walked us through and revealed to me over the past five to seven years.

Since the age of nineteen, when I first accepted Jesus Christ as my Savior, I have been seeking the Lord and listening to and reading books from such great men as Kenneth Copeland, Kenneth Hagin, Creflo Dollar, and Bill Winston. In addition to these four men, there have been many others that have made significant deposits in my life, including my pastor, Pastor Thomas Peetz (who happens to have been my wife's youth pastor when she was growing up). The greatest teachers of all, however, have been the Word of God and the Holy Spirit.

In the summer of 2011 while I was seeking the Lord on this topic, the Lord spoke to me and told me to write a book about it and to name the book *A King's Journey*. From my early thirties, I have known that I was called to business and finances. As I look back to when I was in my twenties, I always felt connected to Joseph in the Bible. For years the Lord would speak to me and reveal things to me from the Scriptures and would specifically use scriptures from Joseph's life to help me. In my early years I would believe God for the things that He was revealing to me. And although it may not seem significant, at the age of thirty I made a six-figure income for the first time. Prior to that, I had never made anywhere near that. But God kept speaking to me, and I kept doing my best to listen. And, over time, He began to expand my vision and my sight, and as I began to see bigger, I began to live in more of what the Scriptures said I already had.

In 2006 Michele and I traveled to Milwaukee and attended one of Brother Copeland's Believers' Conventions. It was during that convention that God first started showing me pictures, images, and revealing concepts to me. From that point forward these pictures and concepts continued to expand in my heart. Looking back at it now, He was revealing many different truths to me that would eventually make up the contents of this book.

The morning I first introduced these concepts and images to our local church, I was getting ready in the bathroom, and I asked the Lord, "Lord, what's up with these images You're giving me?" And you know, He answered me just like that. I heard on the inside, "They are parables, the same way I taught. But they are up-to-date parables, things that people can understand and connect with now." Wow, that blew me away—high-tech analogies for a high-tech generation.

Over the past two years, I have learned not to say no. What I mean by that is, if the Lord is speaking to me about something that is beyond my ability to see, comprehend, or even beyond my ability to currently do, I have learned not to say no. Instead, I have learned to keep quiet and to think about it until I can ask the Lord an intelligent question for further understanding.

When the Lord told me to write this book, I was extremely busy. I had a very demanding job, three kids with active schedules, and a wife that I am still crazy about and love to spend time with. I saw no way I would have any time to sit and write a book. But rather than saying no to the Lord, I said to Him, "Lord, if You want me to write this book—and I believe that You do—You will need to show me how to do it. Thank You for revealing it to me." About three days later a thought from my spirit rose up to my mind, and the words *dictation software* came to me. And I said, "Aha! That's how I will do it." Although I have never written a book before this, it has been one of the easiest things I have never done. It pays to listen to the Lord.

Although I refer to kings and priests, this book has to do with kings. Kings are men and women of God that are called to make enormous amounts of money to establish, build, and finance the Kingdom of God in the earth. In this book you will also learn how to use God's operating system in the earth and get off of the world's operating system. God's operating system is called KOGOS, the Kingdom of God's operating system, and it will change how you view everything.

Finally, this book is written to everyone who desires to fulfill the call of God on his or her life. In addition to many high-tech analogies and pictures, this book truly is an instructional handbook on how to follow the Lord to fulfill what He's called *you* to do. I hope you enjoy this adventure through *A King's Journey*.

Chapter One

KINGS AND PRIESTS

W E SEE EXAMPLES of kings and priests throughout the Bible, especially in the Old Testament. When we look at Revelation 1:5–6, it says, "And from Jesus Christ, who is the faithful witness, and the first begotten of the dead, and *the prince of the kings of the earth.* Unto him that loved us, and washed us from our sins in his own blood, And *hath made us kings and priests* unto God and his Father; to him be glory and dominion for ever and ever. Amen."

The Bible says that Jesus is the Prince of the kings of the earth and that He has made us kings and priests. There has been extensive teaching on the office of the priests over the years. We know from Scripture that we are all priests. We can all share the Word of God, minister to the Lord, and minister to those who God brings across our paths. We can share the love of God with people, and we can lead people to the Lord. In that sense we are all priests.

However, there are those who God has called to the office of the priest. These people are called to be full-time priests. We know them better by Ephesians 4:11–12, "And he gave some, apostles; and some, prophets; and some, evangelists; and some, pastors and teachers; For the perfecting of the saints, for the work of the ministry, and for the edifying of the body of Christ." Although we can all flow in the anointing of God in these areas—and we should!—I believe there is a higher level of anointing that accompanies the position of leadership that is upon the full-time priests. You can pray for somebody in the parking lot, and they can receive healing. However, bring them into a healing service where the Spirit of God is moving on the full-time priest, and often you will experience a greater level of anointing.

In the same manner, we are all called as kings. There is an anointing on all of us to bring in the necessary finances for our lives. This anointing gives us influence and spiritual power to go to work, bring in the spoil, and provide what is needed. Jesus is our Prince, and He has called us all to be kings and priests in the earth. We are part of the family of God, and as such we are royalty. Kings rule and reign; they are not peasants. They are in charge of their kingdom and have the final word in their area of domain. Kings are to rule and reign in the earth under the leadership and example of the Lord Jesus Christ.

As we walk in our kingship there is an anointing on us to bring in finances to the local church in tithes and offerings, which helps build the Kingdom of God. The church needs finances to expand His Kingdom. It's not the priest's job to work and bring in the money; it's the king's job. If you are not in full-time ministry, then you are a king, and God wants to establish your kingship, that you may begin to walk in the fullness of your royalty. In so doing, your financial increase will cause you to have more resources. Your tithe will proportionally grow, and out of your abundance you can bring in offerings to help build the Kingdom.

Although we are all called to be kings, there are some that are called to the office of the king. God has called some men and women in the body of Christ to make enormous amounts of money to finance the Kingdom of God in the earth. With this calling comes an anointing from the Lord, the king's anointing, to get massive amounts of wealth. Why do I use the phrase *office of the king*? It has nothing to do with some fancy title or something to put on a business card; that's just foolishness. I use that phrase to compare and contrast it with the office of the priest, so you will better understand what I mean. We all minister, but some are called to full-time ministry. We all work to bring in finances, but some are called to bring in huge amounts of wealth.

The world has worldly kings that are in charge of businesses, industries, and commerce. They are the millionaires and the billionaires that run things and are in control. These people have power and massive influence to make things go the direction that they want. These people run the media, healthcare, banks, technology, and so forth. They are people of wealth and leadership who decide and influence the future of their businesses and industries. As a result, they impact and influence the lives of thousands and millions.

I believe God is raising up godly kings that love the Lord with all their heart and are committed to Him. I believe that God has strategically placed these kings in positions of leadership and authority in businesses, industries, and commerce in His Kingdom for His purpose. What is God's purpose in calling and anointing kings? To acquire massive amounts of finances and resources in order to establish, build, and advance the

Kingdom of God in the earth. Worldly kings will not do that. They have their own agenda to control resources and people. But that's why God is training up godly kings to acquire wealth, and He has a method of doing it. Surprisingly enough, it's not the same method or system the world uses. God has a system, or a way of doing things. From now on, we are going to refer to this way of doing things as an operating system.

The worldly kings follow the world's operating system, but godly kings need to learn how to follow God's operating system. God's system, or God's way of doing things, has a name; it's called the Kingdom of God Operating System. From now on, we will refer to God's system as *KOGOS*. There have been many godly kings who have tried to make things happen the world's way, and it just won't work right. God wants to teach His kings how to operate His Kingdom principles. With God's anointing upon His kings and the kings following KOGOS, the world doesn't have a chance of staying in control.

We are all called as kings and priests (over our homes and areas of domain). We can all flow in the priest's anointing and can lay hands on the sick and see them recover. We can also flow in the king's anointing and live in an abundance of finances to not only provide for our families but to have an overflow of resources and finances to establish the gospel.

One summer while vacationing in Maine, I was meditating on this topic of kings and priests. I was enquiring of the Lord with the thought that if full-time priests have a higher level of anointing in certain areas of ministry, then there must also be the equivalent anointing for the full-time king to minister in his or her area of domain in business. And in an instant, the Lord showed it to me in His Word.

The priest's anointing is located in Luke 4:18–19. It says, "The Spirit of the Lord is upon me, because he hath anointed me to preach the gospel to the poor; he hath sent me to heal the brokenhearted, to preach deliverance to the captives, and recovering of sight to the blind, to set at liberty them that are bruised, To preach the acceptable year of the Lord." Although we are all called to flow in this anointing, God has called some to the office of the priest, and these full-time priests have a greater level of power that matches the calling that God has placed on them.

The king's anointing is located in Deuteronomy 8:18. It says, "But thou shalt remember the Lord thy God: for it is he that *giveth thee power to get wealth*, that he *may establish his covenant* which he sware unto thy fathers, as it is this day" (emphasis added). Although we are all called to this and are expected to walk in this, God has called and anointed some to the office of the king. These full-time kings have a greater level of power and *kingly anointing* that matches the calling that God has placed on them.

The scripture says that God gives us power. Isn't that another word for *anointing*? And what is the purpose of this anointing? It is to get wealth. Do the full-time priests bear the primary responsibility to get wealth? No. Their primary function as a priest is to minister according to the Scriptures. However, if they are in faith in this area, then they should be walking in the blessing and prosperity of the Lord just like everyone else can.

I am making this distinction for a reason. Deuteronomy 8:18 is the king's anointing. Although we are all called as kings, there are some that are called to be full-time kings, and God has placed a higher level of anointing and power on them to get massive amounts of wealth. The primary purpose for this wealth is to establish His covenant, or in other words, to establish or finance the Kingdom of God in the earth.

As I was meditating this to the Lord, I saw it. When a minister is in his calling and is flowing in the anointing of God, he can do supernatural things. Although we as faith people see it all the time, it is not "natural" for one person to lay hands on someone that is sick and in a moment they become well. That is not natural or normal. This anointing that the minister is operating in allows them to bypass and overcome natural laws. If this is true of the priest's anointing in their function and area of domain, wouldn't it stand to reason that the same is true of the king's anointing?

In other words, if the priest can overcome natural laws as they minister as a priest, then the kings should also be able to flow in the king's anointing and overcome and bypass natural laws in the areas of business and finances.

Let me put it another way. The worldly financial advisors will tell you that if you save and invest x amount on a monthly basis over so many years, you will have the amount of money that you need to buy a house, put kids into college, buy a beach home, or retire comfortably. If you are operating according to only the natural, then these natural laws of time, money, and risk apply to you. In contrast to that, if you as a godly king *choose* a different operating system, one that gives you supernatural power to create and get wealth, than you can override natural laws and collapse the time it takes to get wealth. It's called the king's anointing, and you flow and operate in it just like you would believe God for wisdom or believe God for healing for your child. Kings can operate in the same type of power and anointing that overcomes natural laws, just like priests can when they are ministering. It is the same Holy Spirit, just another aspect of Him for a different calling and purpose.

God revealed this to me through a book called *Heaven Is for Real*. This is the story of a three-year-old boy who went to heaven and came back to talk about it. The boy refers to his father, who is a pastor of a church (a full-time priest). The boy, Colton, describes that he saw Jesus "[shoot] down power on daddy when he's talking."[1] When I read it, I knew this was true, but to hear a little boy describe what he saw really blew me away.

If Jesus "shoots down power" on the priests, then Jesus also "shoots down power" on the kings. *The priest's anointing is supernatural power to preach and minister the gospel to people. The king's anointing is supernatural power to get wealth to finance the gospel for people.* Kings are interested and focused on bringing the finances in; priests are interested and focused on getting the gospel out. Don't try to change them. It's how God wired them. When they work together, the Kingdom of God expands!

Here is what the Spirit of God told me:

> Deuteronomy 8:18 was written for the kings. When you are in the will of God, fulfilling the call He has for you with the goal of establishing His kingdom, He "shoots down power" to you as a king to make it massively simple to create and gather wealth. Deuteronomy 8:18 says He "gives me power." He shoots kingly power or anointing and makes it massively simple to get wealth. As a priest, when you're flowing in the Holy Spirit, it's massively simple to preach and minister healing to the people. There's a flow that's power-filled, and the priests can do things that naturally can't be done because of the power that's on them.

The king can operate in the same way when you're in His will, fulfilling what God has called you to. There's a flow of the Holy Spirit for the king that has anointing and power from Jesus to gather wealth. It's massively simple. Just like the preacher who prays for the sick and they get healed, the king follows the leading of the Holy Spirit in kingly matters, and making money and creating wealth is massively simple, even defies natural laws, like healing defies natural laws for the priests. Jesus "shoots down power" on the kings and makes it massively simple to create and gather huge wealth. The key to the kings is John 15:4–7, "Abide in me, and I [abide] in you."

We have to remember that Jesus is our King *and* our High Priest. If a priest's anointing can heal a sick body, cast out a spirit, and raise the dead (which surpasses and overcomes natural laws), what can a king's anointing do? We have already established that the king's anointing is an anointing for increase to benefit the Kingdom of God on the earth. So what is the issue? If God has called us to be kings, why don't we have a large number of kings moving into big wealth? I think for many of us, if not most of us, we are trying to walk into this promise using man's ways instead of using KOGOS, the Kingdom of God Operating System. We want to fulfill our call and finance the gospel; however, for many of us we are working it the wrong way. When it comes to money and getting wealth, many of us are making our own decisions and doing it man's way, which is the world's system, rather than doing it God's way, which is believing Him for it and allowing the Holy Spirit to direct us and walk us right into it.

Remember, there is an anointing on you to get wealth. How do you access that anointing? Well, how does a full-time priest minister healing? He is in tune with the Holy Spirit and follows His leading when he ministers. When he does that, the anointing of the Holy Spirit is present and accomplishes that which it was sent to do. Hey kings, listen up! There is an anointing on you to get wealth, but you can't do it the old way that you may have been taught. You have to operate in your anointing in the realm of business and finances, similar to how a minister operates and flows in the anointing in a service. It's the same anointing and the same Holy Spirit. I'm not talking about being weird or hokey; I'm talking about being in tune and relying upon the Holy Spirit.

You can have the same type of supernatural results in finances as some of these great men of God have in healing services. You cannot get the wealth God has planned for you to establish His Kingdom in any other way. He sent His power and anointing to you and on you for you to operate in it to fulfill what the anointing was sent to do, which is to get wealth. In this handbook I will walk you through how God taught me and is still teaching me how to flow in the king's anointing.

The Lord's power supersedes and surpasses any other power that's out there. This power that He places on you is not a casual thing. Jesus is *the* King of kings, and it is *the* King's anointing that He places on you. This power does not just marginally surpass other powers; *the* King's power far surpasses any other power that's out there. *The* King's "power" that He places on *His* kings in the earth far, far, far surpasses the power of time, the power of governments, the power of Wall Street, the power of Hollywood, and the power of any other groupings of rich men or countries. This is *the* King of kings' power, the Creator of the universe and of all things.

If you would simply take the time to meditate and give yourself to this truth, it would absolutely change everything for you. If you are a believer, then His power is on you. When you have His power and are following His plan for your life, you are absolutely *invincible* and *unstoppable*. There may be some obstacles that appear to try and thwart the plan of God, but there is no power that can actually stop His power and His plan placed in and on you. When you learn to operate according to God's system (KOGOS), you are unstoppable.

Chapter Two

MY JOURNEY

I ACCEPTED THE LORD in 1989 at the age of nineteen and began to learn what it meant to live by faith. However, my journey as it relates to the topics discussed in this book began in late 1998. The company I was working for went bankrupt, and I was looking for a job. Fortunately I was successful in sales and was offered sales positions by six different companies. They all looked good, and they all told me their companies were tremendous and that I would have great success with them. In the natural, I could have picked any of them, but instead I made the decision to seek God and ask Him which job He had for me. While I was driving back from one of the interviews I was praying and asking the Lord for His direction, and I clearly heard the Lord tell me in my spirit which job to take. I knew that I knew that I had heard Him.

The only issue was that when I spoke to the hiring manager a week later, he informed me the position was put on hold for six months. That really confused me, but the position was not available. I took one of the other positions with a more established company and began to work for them. After about six months, I reached back out to the company that God told me to go to, and they brought me back in and hired me. I have my own will, and I had options. I could have stayed where I was, but it was not what God told me to do. God told me what job to take, so I chose to follow that.

Over the next ten years I enjoyed tremendous success at this company, believing God and giving my best every step of the way. Over the years I went from a sales representative to a manager to a director and then to a regional vice president. There were definitely some bumps along the way and many growing pains that I personally went through.

A couple of times over this ten-year period I got frustrated at some things going on at work and wanted to start looking for a new job. I'm sure this has never happened to you! On these occasions I would speak to my wife, Michele, and tell her that I was frustrated and that I wanted to start looking for a new job. She patiently listened to me, and when I was done ranting she would ask me one simple question: "Did God tell you to leave?" Don't you know, this was not what I wanted to hear! I was the one working, I was frustrated, and I wanted a new job. Did you notice the common theme? As I thought about her question each time, I realized that she was right. If I left, I would have been leaving on my own. I would have been leaving a place that God told me to go. God was teaching me an important lesson: *No matter how good something looks someplace else, if you go someplace God did not tell you to go, it is a dangerous place.*

So I stayed, because I knew God told me to take this job, and I knew God had not told me to leave. Although I did not realize it at the time, these were seasons of development and preparation for me. They were times where God was maturing me in areas and strengthening my character. To put it bluntly, God was making me do the push-ups to develop muscles in areas where I was weak. If God has called you to take the hill, but you don't have the strength and the stamina to even make it halfway up the mountain, will you succeed and fulfill in the thing that God has called you to? The answer is no, you won't. *If you don't do the work in the preparation phase, you will not be ready for the promotion phase.*

At the time there were many new telecom start-up companies I could have gone to. I stayed with this company, and over a ten-year period I had developed a very successful track record of a being a sales leader within this organization. At this point the company I was working for had grown significantly. We went from being a little start-up company to being listed on the Fortune 1000. We grew to this size from a combination of both organic growth and acquisitions.

One of the major acquisitions the company had made literally doubled the geographic coverage in the US. It was a substantial expansion with the expectation that it would become a huge revenue-producing part of the company. After about a year or so the largest region within this newly acquired company was just floundering. They did not know our company, our sales process, or how to get things done within our organization. They had brought in outside leadership to run this region, and it was just not working. As such, the executive team came to the realization that the only way to turn this large region around was to put one of their own seasoned veterans in to run this region.

Every year, our regional offices would hold a large customer event at a high-end restaurant. Typically, one or two of the executives would come in for that event and meet and mingle with our customers. We were having one of these events, and our CEO flew in for it. Within ten minutes of the event the CEO pulled me aside and began to talk to me about making a move for the company and taking this critical position in Texas. The CEO offered me a tremendous position within the company. With this promotion came a significant six-figure income and stock options. At the time the housing market had dropped, and we were upside down on our home. In addition, we did not have 20 percent to put down on a new house in Texas. Slightly embarrassed, I told him I would need a significant amount of money to make all that work, at least eighty thousand dollars after taxes. He said that the company would bonus that to me, and it would take care of the loss at home and the down payment.

If that was not good enough, the CEO then told me that when I turned the region around, he would promote me to the executive team and make me the president of the southwest region. He knew my wife, Michele, pretty well and told me to talk to her about it and get back to him.

I walked away from the conversation in a bit of a daze. This type of thing had not happened to me before. The reality was, I felt like I had been stuck in middle management for many years, and this was my chance to move into an upper management position with a clear path to be an executive by the age of forty-one. The CEO made it very clear that he really wanted me, and I have to admit it was nice to be wanted. The first chance I got, I called Michele and told her what happened. She wanted the blow by blow of the conversation. I quickly realized that I could probably ask for whatever I wanted and they would give it to me. After a couple of days, I called the CEO back and told him we would proceed with the interview process and see where things would take us.

Since I had first taken the job ten years earlier, I began believing God for the position they were offering me. I did not necessarily ask God if it was His will; I just put my faith to work and began believing and declaring it. Now here it was! This must be God! In addition, I always told my wife that if we were to ever move, I would want to move to Texas. What's not to love about Texas? Although we have no family there, we knew we would go to Eagle Mountain Church and be part of Kenneth Copeland Ministries. The cost of homes and living was much less than that of New England. Check! My oldest daughter owned a horse, and I knew Texas had that covered. Check! My youngest daughter could play basketball, and I even found a hockey organization for my son to play at. Check! My kids would get plugged into the youth group and children's ministry at Eagle Mountain. Check! Texas even had the Dallas Cowboys! I'm a Patriots fan, but have always liked the Cowboys. I would be making way more money, get a large signing bonus, and reduce my expenses. *This must be God!* I thought.

Wow, naturally speaking it was everything I had been believing for, and it seemed like the Lord set this up and did this for us. Michele and I were praying and seeking the Lord, but we just didn't seem to find an answer either way. I continued with the interview process and even put a formal business plan together to present on my final interview. On the day I was to conduct my final interview, I woke up early and drove to the airport to fly out to California. When I landed in Chicago for my connecting flight, I called Michele, and she told me she had a dream the night before. I have learned over the years that when Michele tells me she has a dream I need to listen closely. I don't get dreams from the Lord very often, but that is one way that God communicates to Michele.

As she told me the entire dream, I immediately knew what it meant. The Lord was communicating to us that although this looked like an amazing opportunity, it did not come from Him. In the end it would tear our marriage and family apart. I knew that I knew that God had said no and that this was not *His plan.* I even asked, "Why should I even continue with the interview process then?" But as Michele and I discussed that, we thought it would be wise to finish the interview process. After all, how would I tell these executives that my wife had a "bad dream" and that I would not be taking the job? That would have gone over like a lead balloon.

There are many things that we should just keep to ourselves. This is often why some people get tagged as a weirdo or a flake. Don't be one of those people. You will lose your influence into the lives of non-Christians. If they don't respect you, they will not hear you. I'm not saying not to do what's right; I'm saying be selective in what you tell certain people. Jesus did not tell everything to everyone. He spoke in parables to the large crowds but yet gave more detail to the disciples. Know your audience and deliver a message that is appropriate to them.

I completed the interview process, and Michele and I took twenty-four hours to talk and pray everything through. Clearly God had spoken, and He did not orchestrate this turn in the road. I professionally and respectfully thanked them for the offer and told them that although the opportunity was tremendous and that I was incredibly honored that they offered it to me, the move would be too great of a sacrifice to my family; therefore I had to decline. So I stayed in my position, because God did not tell me to go.

It was business as usual for me for about three more months. After this short amount of time I started to become dissatisfied with my position. I would continue to work hard and give my best, but I had something scratching at me on the inside. After about six more months of this, I began spending more time with one of my business contacts who was also a Christian and newer friend. As I spent time with him I just felt this draw or connection to him and was trying to figure out what it meant. Was God connecting us because we were going to start a business together? We talked about that, but that wasn't it. My friend could sense that I was dissatisfied and had reached the end of my season with the company I had been with. The company had been very good to me, but I knew on the inside that my time was coming to an end.

The company my friend worked for was looking for a vice president of sales. He made the introduction, and we had several meetings and interviews over a two-month period. Throughout this process God was showing me exactly what needed to be done to expand this business and make it extremely successful. It was almost the identical situation as the job in Texas. In both cases, the problems and the solutions were very clear to me. I wrote business plans that addressed the problems and put the company on the right path from a growth and revenue expansion perspective. Michele pointed that out to me. We both thought that was a little too peculiar. We were both praying and talking on a regular basis about the possibility of this position. In the natural, things look pretty good, but we still were not sure and did not have a clear direction on the matter. Once again, God gave my wife a dream. As she was telling me the dream, again I clearly knew that this position I was considering was a "no." So I stayed in my position, because God did not tell me to go.

A short time after this experience this same friend called me about a start-up high-tech company that he was doing some consulting for. I knew absolutely nothing about what this company did. I knew nothing about the incredible innovation of the technology. I was a telecommunications veteran and knew nothing about the data storage and data protection industry. But as my friend began to talk to me about it, something on the inside lit up. This had not happened with either of the other two opportunities. So I began the conversations and interviews with the CEO of this company. The more I spoke to the CEO, the more I felt right on the inside. This was a process of conversations with the company, conversations with my wife, Michele, and prayer seeking the Lord and inquiring of His plans.

After a duration, I knew that I knew on the inside that this was the opportunity that God had orchestrated for me to walk in. The previous two experiences I went through helped me incredibly in the interview process and compensation negotiation for the position that God actually had planned for me. We came to an agreement; they offered me the position of VP of the northeast, and I took the job. Notice that although the other positions were not for me, God had me go through the experience of them in order to prepare me for what He *did* want me to do.

In the other opportunities, I had a full-blown business plan prepared but no witness on the inside that I was the one to take the job and implement the plan. With this opportunity I put a very, very basic plan together, because the reality was I knew *nothing* about this industry or the technology I was going to be selling, or even the technology that our stuff was replacing. What I did know was that I had a witness that this was right, and the Holy Spirit was urging and nudging me along to take this job. So I followed that. I did not have the big-picture plan, but I did have direction from the Lord: "Take the job."

Throughout this entire process I found myself praying, reading Scripture, and going back to two books that have helped me incredibly over the years. The two books are both written by Kenneth E. Hagin and are titled *How You Can Be Led by the Spirit of God* and *Plans, Purposes, and Pursuits*. As a matter of fact, every time I had to make an important decision, I found myself rereading the highlighted sections of this book, praying in the Spirit, and then listening for answers.

I gave my formal resignation with notice to the company I had been at for almost twelve years. Several of the executives called me and asked if there was anything they could do to keep me with them. I did not even entertain the idea. I thanked them for everything they had done for me and left on great terms with that company. That was where I grew up, matured, and developed tremendous skills and character that would sustain me for the next season that God had planned for me. Although God knew, little did I know the chain of events that were about to unfold in this new season of my life.

The day before I was to start my new job we were attending Sunday morning service, and God spoke to Michele about what God was doing with me at this new company. Michele does not normally write stuff like this down; I am the one that does that. But Michele knew in her heart that she would have been in disobedience if she did not write down what God was telling her. So she obeyed and wrote it down.

Here's what she wrote on October 10, 2010—10/10/10—the day before I started:

> The door has been opened. The door has been opened. The door has been opened by *Me*. What you have been sensing these past few months has been preparing you for what's about to happen. Walk through the door. I opened that door just for you. Not because someone else wouldn't walk through it; it's because I created for you to walk through it, and you said yes. It is I that brought you here to the door for more than you even have seen or even realize. I haven't unveiled it all to you because your mind would get in the way. Just continue to walk where I tell you. I will reveal it to you as the time comes. Just remember how I led you here (through the leading of my Spirit) and continue to follow that. My hand is on this for more than you even see at this time. Continue to be you, do what you do, and watch what will begin to unfold because *My* hand is on it.

Little did I know how absolutely critical it was that Michele obeyed the Lord when she wrote this down for me. There was some turbulent weather coming, and I would refer back to this often to keep me on the right course. Without it, I might have forgotten what the Lord had said to me and gone off course.

Chapter Three

NEW SEASON

THE HIGH TECHNOLOGY industry for the most part consists of two hot beds in the country where most of technology innovation happens, Silicon Valley and Boston. In Boston many of the high-tech companies find themselves in the 128 Belt in Massachusetts, which is a suburb of Boston. This is where my new company was headquartered. They were what we called an early-stage tech start-up company.

Early-stage start-ups are unlike anything you have probably ever experienced. People that thrive in early stage start-ups are cut from a different cloth. They have a "whatever it takes" attitude and will put it all on the line to succeed. I would compare these people to pilgrims or pioneers, people that are willing to cut down the very first tree and make a path and then a community where nothing existed previously. Early-stage starts are for the true business warriors. You don't know what you don't know. You have no customers, no process, no marketing; just a really cool idea or technology that you think people will want to buy. The executives have a plan, but when you go to market you have to constantly make adjustments on the fly. There's nothing like it.

In addition to that, although we were an early-stage start-up, we were in a very established industry with dominant players and established technologies that customers were used to buying. Our technology was what we called a new category. It wasn't faster, better, or cheaper than what was already out there; it was fundamentally, totally different. Our technology replaced five to six other existing technologies.

So here was my challenge: I was a total outsider to this industry. Not only did I not know anything about our technology, but I knew nothing about the five or six technologies that we were replacing. Each of these technologies represented huge divisions with specialists in each of these individual segments. The CEO apparently really liked me and hired me. Honestly, I had no idea what the Lord had gotten me into.

Before I started my job Michele and I had thoroughly talked this through. We estimated that it would take about six months of real hard work to get over the hump. Little did I know it wasn't a hump, but it was actually Mount Everest! I was literally working fourteen-hour days for the first six months of my job. The first twelve hours were allocated to doing work for the company and going to see customers. After a long day of work, I than came home and put in another two hours at night going online and watching technology training videos from the competition. Almost every day I would hear acronyms of things I had no idea of, and since we had no training department I went searching online to first understand what the technology did and then later how it interacted with all of the other technologies customers were buying.

Imagine doing a puzzle in the dark with a flashlight. You figure out how a couple of pieces fit together, and then you realize the puzzle is bigger than you thought. Every time you think you've got it, your flashlight puts out more light, and you realize that the puzzle is bigger than you thought. After months of working on this puzzle, imagine someone walking in and turning on the ceiling light, and you now finally see that the puzzle covers the entire floor of the room you are standing in. This is what it felt like for me, and I had to believe God to learn every piece of the puzzle and how each piece fit together.

Although I was the area VP of sales, for the first three months I said absolutely nothing on customer appointments. My engineer would do both the sales presentation and the technical discussion. As I sat there, I would document all the acronyms I was clueless about. As time went on and I did my extra homework at night, pieces of the puzzle began to make sense. It was a progressive thing for me. It did not all happen in one shot; I worked hard at it every day and just kept chipping away at it. Somewhere around the beginning of my fourth month I had learned enough to give the canned presentation. No extras, no commentary, just the plain vanilla presentation. After another month, I begin delivering a better presentation with some commentary and could answer a couple of questions. Additionally, as the VP of the northeast and first sales person, I was running a ton of sales appointments while interviewing other candidates for other regions.

Let me pause here for a moment and make a point that needs to be made. As Christians, there seems to be a wide range of thinking when it comes to what your part is and what God's part is in this equation. I know plenty of Christians who think that all they have to do is pray and believe God and that's it. Some of these same people seem to think that if it doesn't come easy, it's not of God. I think these people are just plain lazy and hide behind "being in faith." The Scriptures teach that faith without works is dead. A clearer version of this scripture is "faith without *corresponding action* yields no results" (James 2:20, author's paraphrase). In spite of this truth, how many Christians follow God and then get to the point where they have to put in the extra work and go; "Hey, I don't want to do these push-ups; I don't want to do the hard work. Must not be God," and they take themselves out of the plan of God. God had clearly brought me to this company, but I had to work extra hard to get myself to a place of knowledge, skill, and development where He could begin to use me.

All I can say is, I had no idea I was going to have to do "ten thousand push-ups" to get myself to a point where I could be successful. It was like God told me I was going to be a soldier but then sent me to boot camp to prepare me first. Although I have never gone to a military boot camp, I went to a business boot camp. I went into a situation with all of the raw skills needed, but there were a whole bunch of things that needed to be added to what I had in order to complete me and prepare me for what I was called to do.

About five months into my new career, the CEO hired an executive responsible for sales operations. Both of these gentlemen were massively successful in their own rights, having built and sold numerous companies prior to this company. These executives were the "generals" in this industry; they were hard-core successful entrepreneurs.

This new executive already had a proven sales formula that worked. It included the right sales profile, the right people, and the right go-to-market methodology that was tested and proven. When he came in, he observed the business for about thirty days before making any changes. After that evaluation period, he began to make his changes, and one of those first changes began with me. He called me into his office, sat me down, and began to explain how he was going to run sales as the sales manager for a couple of months and that he wanted me to move into a sales representative position. In that ten-minute conversation, I was demoted from the VP of the northeast and moved into a sales rep position. On top of that, he was not the person that hired me, and I did not have the years of industry knowledge and experience that he normally brings into his organization. He normally hired the "Navy SEALS" of this industry, and it remained to be seen what I was. He offered me this new position and told me to let him know if I wanted to stay on board. I swallowed hard.

I walked out of that meeting in a total fog. What just happened to me?

All those years of hard work moving up the management ranks, and in thirty days all of it was lost. What was he actually planning? Did I make a mistake by coming here? Was I going to lose my job? If I lost that, would I lose my house? It was like a swarm of bees in my head, just buzzing around with all of these questions and doubt.

Although there was a storm going on in my head where I was being bombarded with outside thoughts of doubt, I have learned not to follow the outside thoughts that come into my head but rather to check my spirit and to only follow that. As I took a walk outside, I prayed and checked my spirit, and although my head was noisy and stormy, when I checked my spirit it was blue skies and calm waters on the inside. There was a storm raging on the outside, but on the inside it was calm waters for as far as I could see. No anxiety, no doubt, no commotion, no fear, no concern; just calm waters and blue skies. Although I did not understand what happened or what was going to happen, I knew in my heart I was going to be all right.

I called Michele, my life partner, my confidant, my helpmate, and just all-around amazing woman of God. I told her the story of what just happened, and we talked things through for quite a while. And, of course, we prayed together. Although I was totally confused as to what was happening and none of this made any sense to me whatsoever, I had a total peace about it on the inside and knew God would take care of me. I went back in to meet with this executive and told him that I was on board and would give him my best in this new sales position.

Having been in management for the last twelve years, I knew what was going on. When you're trying to build a sales organization, you don't start by hiring the newbies in the industry. You go hire the seasoned professionals that have already been successful time and time again in the industry. I had five months under my belt, a far cry from the seasoned professionals he normally hired. I'm not sure he knew it, but the technology was just starting to make sense to me. Some of the puzzle pieces were starting to come together, and although I definitely did not have it all, I was beginning to see the whole picture and how to put it together.

Several new sales teams were hired to join the company, and one of those teams was put right in the best part of the territory to cover the metro Boston market, which was where I was spending most of my time. I was asked to cover the surrounding states, which were much more remote. The best accounts in the most concentrated area were given to the new team, and I was given everything else. Needless to say, my confidence was shaken to the core.

In addition to the things I knew naturally, because I was in tune with the Lord I would pick up on conversations happening in the spirit. I knew the only reason I wasn't fired was because the CEO hired me and would not allow it to happen. So rather than be fired, I was moved to a sales rep position and would quickly sink or swim. I knew the thinking was that in ninety days I probably would not make it, and I could just be let go and move on. If you are in business, you know that this is normal and common. If you have a formula that is proven and works, you implement it and execute it. I understood what was happening, and no one was doing anything wrong per se. The only part that didn't make any sense was how this all related to me. The Lord brought me here, the Lord led me to this place at this time and with this specific company.

The ensuing two months were the most difficult time in *my entire life.* I felt like I was hanging over a cliff, holding on to a rope with every ounce of strength in me. The rope, of course, was the Lord Jesus. In the natural, I had no other footing to stand on. I felt completely exposed and absolutely vulnerable. I knew that if I did not perform I was falling off the cliff. Outside thoughts of losing my job, losing our house, and taking a major financial setback were bombarding my mind like waves of the sea crashing on the shore.

I kept going back to this one question, though: *Who brought me here?* I did not bring myself here, this I knew for sure. *The Lord is the One who led me here and told me to walk through this door.* Every single day I would reread what the Lord spoke to Michele and told her to write down for me the day before I started this job. All I can say is thank God that she obeyed the Lord and wrote it down. I'm not sure what would have happened to me if she had not. Due to my thought process at the time, there were parts of what the Lord said that didn't make much sense to me. But I knew that He had brought me here and that He would take care of me. I trusted the Lord.

I stood on one particular scripture that was the only thing that would allow me to breathe and would settle my heart when the anxiety tried to overwhelm me. Proverbs 3:4–5 (NKJV) says, "Trust in the Lord with all your heart, and lean not on your own understanding. In all your ways acknowledge Him and He will direct your path."

It was like air to me, an oxygen tank sustaining me in a whirlwind of a storm. The pressure became so bad that one day Michele walked in on me while in my home office and found me crying. I still get emotional when I talk about this period in my life. I had never been in a place like this. All these years Michele had only known me as a positive, motivated leader who had always been successful. I was on the verge of being broken. Michele even asked me if I just wanted to go find a new job. It would have been really easy to go get a new job in the field I just came from. Heck, I probably could have gone back to my former employer; they would have taken me back in a heartbeat. But with tears in my eyes I told her no. I knew that God had brought me here, that I did not bring myself, and I would not leave.

The Lord was with me every step of the way. I was clinging on to Him for dear life, and He had me securely in His hands and would not let me fall. Even though nothing made any sense to me, He brought me here because He already had a plan worked out from before the foundation of the world.

And then something happened. It seemed like one day everything just clicked and started making sense. About thirty to forty-five days into this ninety-day period, the light came on. I saw and knew exactly what I needed to do to be successful. Prior to this it was like a mystery that I was trying to figure out. I had continually been asking the Lord to reveal the full picture to me and to give me the wisdom I needed. And then one day…I just got it. Somebody turned on all the lights, and the pieces all fell into place; and I saw the whole picture.

It was our second quarter, and as a company we had revenue projections that we absolutely had to hit. The company committed to do $800,000 in revenue to the board of directors. I had already closed two deals totaling $223,000 for the quarter, but the company was only at $600,000 in revenue up until the very last day of the quarter. I had been working on another deal, and toward the end of the day, on the last day of the quarter, I closed my third deal, worth $215,000. This not only put me well over my quota, but it also pushed the company just over the committed $800,000 in revenue to hit our objectives. As a company, we did it! But let's be honest about what happened here—the Lord did it. He already had these deals prepared for me. I just had to do my part and work them. And in a very short amount of time, I went from the *company zero* to the *company hero*.

I had become the number one rep in the company. But more importantly, the Lord had given me the wisdom needed to sustain success. In the business world, they would say that I figured out a repeatable sales process. That's true. But the wisdom didn't come from me; it came from the Lord, and I had it. It was as if I had conquered the world. I went from being pushed aside in preference to all of the proven successful sales teams to being the main attraction. Now when I would walk into the office, it seemed like everyone wanted to talk to me. This was definitely not happening the few months before! Two weeks later they asked me to teach the sales process in a company-wide training that they were conducting. Oh, the irony of it all!

The following quarter was the same type of thing. The company's revenue target was $1,500,000, and I closed three deals totaling $531,000 for that quarter. The last quarter of 2011, we had a company goal of $2,500,000, which we surpassed! I closed several deals for over $1,200,000. As new teams came on, I was consistently contributing one-third to one-half of the company revenues. It made no sense! I was putting up huge numbers, while the pros being hired were really struggling to close deals.

In a twist of events, a few of the hired gun sales teams that were brought in had made the decision to leave the company. I don't know exactly why they did. The only thing I can think of was that this was a much more difficult sale to figure out. It's always easier to go back to what you know.

I had very quickly become the rep that the company was modeling the sales organization after. At one point they had all the senior sales executives around the world at headquarters, and they asked me to come in and teach them the best-practice sales process that I followed.

Wait a second. How did this happen? Who turned on the lights? How did I all of a sudden have so much favor, recognition, and reward? In the span of six months I went from the guy that was a sliver away from being fired to the number one sales guy in the company. I had influence into what the company should and shouldn't do in the field. And oh the money! I made *way* more money in this position as a rep than I ever did as a regional vice president, with far less travel and way more flexibility with my schedule.

This was what God had planned for me, and I could have easily missed it. I could have left when it got really hard. What gave me the confidence to stay during a massively difficult and naturally stressful time? "As many as are led by the Spirit of God, they are the sons of God" (Rom. 8:14). I reminded myself that I did not bring myself to this company but that the Lord Himself led me here. Therefore my confidence and faith were intact.

As I went back and reread what God told me, I began to see things from a different perspective. God knew that I would have never come to this company as a sales rep. At the time, having a title and being in management was still important to me. God also knew that I needed a five-month head start on learning the fundamentals of the technology before the real pressure came. But I had to put in the extra time and hard work to educate myself. God also knew that the CEO had to be the one to hire me and not someone else, which is why I was hired five months earlier. And finally, He knew that there would come a point in time that it would get so difficult and the pressure so strong that if I did not have the promise of God spoken to me *written down* for me to read over and over and over again I might have allowed myself to be taken out of my divine position because of outside pressures. Instead, when it got really hard, I didn't leave.

I have learned through the years, when God brings you to a place, stay unless He tells you otherwise. Remember, God does not live in time; we do. He sees the end from the beginning and has everything all planned out. These changes did not catch Him by surprise. How could they? Earth exists in time, but the Lord of all eternity does not. He knows the end from the beginning. No, this was all orchestrated by Him, and I had stayed the course.

How critical is it that you *know that you know* you are in the plan of God and not *your* own plan? If I had taken this job on my own instead of allowing the Lord to lead me to it, would I have had the confidence to stay the course in the face of a massive storm? No way.

As I have taken the time to look back and think through this journey that God walked me through, there are so many things and I have learned. They are the things that I have documented in this book, the book *the Lord told me* to write.

First of all, God loves you and has a far better plan for your life than anything you could ever do on your own. His plan is all connected, like a chain of events or like a set of dominoes that are strategically placed, one domino connected to another domino. I have learned to take my hands off of the decision wheel for my life and to totally and completely trust in Him, to follow His leading no matter where He takes me, because it's already predetermined to be successful.

My journey is far from over. But what I have learned thus far, He instructed me to write in this book. Although the name of the book is *A King's Journey*, the subtitle is called *A Handbook for Fulfilling the Call of God for Your Life*. He has an amazing plan for your life. Trust Him to walk you through it.

Chapter Four

THE KING'S ANOINTING

OVER THE PAST several years I have known in my heart that God had called me to be a king. I had been studying along the lines of kings and priests and was inquiring of the Lord to speak to me about it. In early 2010 God spoke clearly to me on two occasions within two weeks of each other. Here's what He said to me about my inquiries regarding the office of the king.

> March, 2010: In the middle of a concert, Deuteronomy 8:18 went off in my spirit. All at once, I knew that with the Lord's hand upon me to gather and create, that when He was personally involved with me to gather wealth, that it would be massively easy. When He placed His anointing upon me to create wealth and to gather wealth...it would be as easy as my job at my current company [previous job where I was the regional vice president]. My job is easy; I know His blessing is on me at my job. I take time to think and to pray, and answers come. Things just work for me, and I perform at a high level. Deuteronomy 8:18 went off in me, and in an instant I knew that with His personal involvement and with His anointing on me to create and gather wealth...it would be as easy as my job, that this would be the easiest thing I have ever done and that it would be impossible for me to fail. As I stay close to Him, I would create massive amounts of wealth, and...it would be massively easy because He was in it with me.

> April, 2010: During Wednesday night worship service, in an instant the Lord Jesus showed me how big *He* was, and as my Lord, creating and gathering and transferring wealth was ridiculously easy. I had been asking myself the question of, Is there any greater man or groupings of men or even groupings of countries that had stronger financial minds or financial plans that could be on the same level as the Lord? And in an instant,

the Lord showed me who *He* was and how [with] *Him with me* no one could stop us from the opposing kingdom. That these men, these groupings of rich men were just that—mere men. He created the universe. He created man. He put all of the wealth and resources in the earth according to His good pleasure. He is the Lord. With Him as my only business partner, my wealth-creating, wealth-gathering, wealth-transferring partner, there are *no limits*. It is time to establish His covenant, His kingdom, and finance His Word in the earth, to seek and save the lost, for the time is upon us. I need to be about my Father's business.

When God spoke these things to me on these two separate occasions, it totally blew me away. I have reread these words many, many times and have meditated on these words to get them in my heart. But there was one saying that always seemed to puzzle me as I would reread what God spoke to me. He said, "*When* He placed His anointing upon me to create wealth and to gather wealth...it would be easy." Why was it written in this tense? I could never figure that out. As I pondered this, I would ask myself, *Isn't His anointing already on me? If it is, then why did the Lord speak to me in that tense?*

In the fall of 2011 I was thinking about the past two quarters and how God took me from a place where I was about to lose my job to that of being extremely successful. What changed during that timeframe? And then I saw it! I remember telling Michele for several months that something was different with me, that something had come on me that I had never experienced before. I didn't quite know what it was, but I would say to her, "Honey, there is something on me that I have never experienced before. I don't know what it is, but the only way I could *not* be massively successful would be to totally walk away from God." Whatever this *thing* was, was pushing me forward and propelling me upward.

The best way I can describe it is to think of a fan that you have in your house, but imagine that this fan is the size of a ten-story building and pointed upward to the sky. Now imagine yourself in a field in front of this fan with an open parachute on, and then somebody turns this massive fan on. That is literally what I felt like. The parachute was not slowing down my descent, but rather the massive power of this fan pointed to the sky caught my parachute and propelled me into the sky with force and power. Never in my life had I felt anything like it. This thing that came on me was pushing me and propelling me into massive success and huge amounts of money.

This thing that had come on me was the king's anointing. I believe it came on me in May 2011. Up until that point I was operating in the *blessing* of God upon my life. Proverbs 10:22 says, "The blessing of the LORD, it maketh rich, and he addeth no sorrow with it." The blessing of God is available to all tithers, and we were enjoying a healthy six-figure income from the blessing. But when God spoke to me in March 2010, He was referring to the *king's anointing*, which had not been placed upon me at that time. That was the reason it was written in that tense. He was telling me, "Hey, something new, really big, and important is coming on you very soon. Get ready for it! When it comes on you, you will be able to do things you never thought you could ever do in the realm of finances."

I don't know why He called me to this; I just know that He has. The purpose for this anointing (the king's anointing) is to get massive wealth in order to establish the Kingdom of God in the earth. I can honestly tell you this: prior to 2006, I would make my own financial decisions and ask God to bless it. I have finally come to a place in my life where I refuse to make any important decisions. I have disciplined myself to only act upon what the Holy Spirit shows me and tells me to do. I love everyone and will listen to what people have to say, but I will immediately go to the Lord with it. If the Holy Spirit tells me to do it, I do it. If He says nothing, I leave it alone and let it float on by. I believe that if I had never gotten to this place in my life, God would never have put the king's anointing on me. I would have been called to it but never chosen for it. In John 5:19, Jesus said, "The Son can do nothing of himself, but what he seeth the Father do: for what things soever he doeth, these also doeth the Son likewise." If this worked for Jesus, it will work for you and I. If Jesus followed this principle and disciplined Himself in this area to live this way, how much more should we?

There have been many books written and preached regarding full-time ministry. Often it is said or suggested from the pulpit that being in full-time ministry is doing the ultimate for God, that there is nothing higher or better than separating and consecrating your life to full-time ministry. For those that God has called to do that, I would totally agree. For the 1 percent to 3 percent of the population that God has called to be in full-time ministry, that is the ultimate—*for them.*

Because I've heard things said over the years along these lines, it seeped into my thinking that unless I was in full-time ministry, I was some how a slightly less important vessel in the Kingdom of God. That is just not true. The highest calling for you as an individual is to fulfill the call of God on *your* life. How can being in full-time ministry be the ultimate if God did not call you to it? That would be unfair of God. Your ultimate in life is to find out what *you* are called to and then ask the Lord to show you how to get started with His plan for your life.

Chapter Five

THE EARLY YEARS

ICHELE AND I got married on November 6, 1993. We grew up in the same neighborhood about eight blocks away from each other and never met. During my grammar school years one of her childhood friends was my immediate neighbor. Michele would hang out there, but we never played together or spoke to each other. By the time we reached high school three of my closest friends lived within one block of Michele's house. I hung out there all the time. We would play basketball, ride bikes, and walk to the local parks close by. All those years (about thirteen years' worth) we played in the same neighborhoods and went to the same high school and never met or spoke. In high school I even dated one of her friends for a little bit, and her best friend went on a date with one of my very close friends; still, no conversations between us.

Michele's mother got saved when Michele was two years old. She grew up as a Christian, went to church, Sunday school, and a private Christian school. As a freshman she went to one of the public high schools in our city, where I attended. She always knew the Lord was real but really didn't know who she was in Christ. Because of that, she had a low self-esteem. Add to that high school peer pressure, and she slowly drifted away from the Lord. Although she generally had a pretty good high school experience, there were definitely some difficult times due to some of the decisions she had made.

I, on the other hand, was a very good heathen! I played varsity football where I was a co-captain of the team. I also played varsity hockey. My friends and I were pretty popular, and if you asked us that's what we would have told you! We were the jocks, and we loved it. To say we were arrogant, brash, and cocky would have been an understatement.

After high school graduation I went to a business college in Massachusetts. In addition to playing on the college hockey team, a bunch of friends got together, and we started a new fraternity chapter on campus. I had the "work hard, play hard" mentality. Whether it was hockey, studying, or just plain partying, I did it 100 percent. As my freshman year ended and I went home for summer break, I found myself drinking and partying more than I had ever done. By the middle of summer, my Friday and Saturday night weekends of partying began to start on Thursday nights and then Wednesday nights. I even got a tattoo on my leg of a devil hockey player. My mother loved that one! I got to a point where I was partying and getting drunk four nights a week. And here was the crazy part—the more I partied, the emptier I felt.

A year earlier my mother had been diagnosed with breast cancer, and it was a pretty emotional time in our life. I loved my mother; she was and is an amazing mother (and grandmother). We were all raised as good Catholics. But when my mother was diagnosed with breast cancer, one of her friends gave her a book by Gloria Copeland on healing. I am thrilled to say that my mother is still with us today, alive and doing well. At the time, though, I did not realize what was really going on. I remember thinking to myself that this must be what people do when they reach their forties; they read the Bible. Pretty funny, huh?

That summer, my mother started to attend healing services that were being held at a different type of church than I was use to. On a Wednesday night in late July 1989, I came home from work and got into a little tiff with my mother regarding college. I went into my room, closed the door, and just totally broke down and could not stop crying. I didn't know what was happening, but I knew my life was totally empty. And the more I partied, the lonelier and more empty I felt. My mother walked in a few minutes later and put her arms around me. She then told me how much she loved me and asked me to go to the church service that night. I was supposed to party with my friends, but something inside of me told me to go with my mom, so I said I would. After I said that, it's like hope entered into my life, and I was able to stop sobbing.

I called my friends and told them I could not make it, and I went off to church with my mom. Here I am in this huge church and the band starts playing, and people start dancing, singing, and raising their arms in the air. To say I was a little freaked out would be an understatement. When I first got there I kept looking around to see if anyone would recognize me. Yes, I was pretty vain. But as the service continued and the worship continued, my heart began to open up to God.

I don't know quite how to describe it, but it seemed to me that in an instant I just knew that Jesus was real. He was no longer the baby Jesus in a manger, the stained glass window in a Catholic church or part of something religious that I grew up with. I knew that I knew that Jesus was real. Although I did not answer an altar call, I sat in my seat and I said to Jesus for the first time, "I know that you are real, and I need you in my life." The best way I can describe it was that another realm of reality became real to me; *He* was made real to me. That night changed the direction of my life forever.

I accepted the Lord into my life about a month before I went back to college for my sophomore year. During that brief time while I got saved and was still at home for summer break I made one Christian friend, was given a couple of books by the Copelands, and went back to school. I had changed big time but was still figuring out what had happened to me and what I had done. My hockey teammates and my fraternity brothers knew something had changed.

My next three years of college would be very different than my first year. Did I get teased at times? Sure I did. However, with many of them they would tease me to have fun, but then they would come find me one on one to ask me a ton of questions about God. I led a handful of people to the Lord during college. I was pretty bold about my faith—I'm sure at times too bold. My college roommate that I had roomed with the year before was Jewish. When we came back to room together for our sophomore year I went from his party buddy to his Jesus freak roommate! After all, a month earlier we were smoking pot at a Ziggy Marley concert. A month later I show up a born-again, on-fire, loud and proud Christian.

His girlfriend at the time was a backslidden Christian. We would talk about the Lord for hours as she slept over in our dorm room. I had a lot of zeal and passion but very little wisdom and skill with people. I definitely made some mistakes along the way, but God helped me every step of the way through this time in my life.

Once I became a Christian, for the most part I stopped dating. I had a lot of reprogramming to do in my mind. When you are used to eating ice cream all the time and you want to stop, the first thing you need to do is stay away from the ice cream parlor. Although my spirit was now saved, my hormones were used to getting what they wanted. I had some major strongholds in my life that I had to take authority over. You have to reprogram your thinking to think about the right kind of stuff. This was probably the most difficult thing I had to do. However, I am happy to report that the Word of God is stronger then any problems you may be facing.

You have to work at renewing your mind with the Word of God. It will change any area in your life that you need changing.

During summer and winter breaks I would come back home to spend time with my family. I remember one day driving around our hometown and asking the Lord who my wife was. I was driving down Bridge Street in Manchester, New Hampshire, and He answered me and told me her name was Michele. The only Michele I could think of was a girl I used to play kickball with in grammar school. I knew it was not her and kind of dismissed the conversation.

After I graduated from college, I came back home to get settled and began my working career. During that summer I walked into a local bank and met with the branch manager to get a car loan. That particular branch happened to be the branch that Michele worked at. After I left the branch manager ran up to Michele and told her that she had just met a male version of her and that if she could pick anyone for her it would be me. Michele's response was, "No way!" You see, at that time, Michele had recently come back to the Lord and made things right with Him. She had just broken up with a guy she had been dating for over two years and had rededicated her life to the Lord. And, of course, she knew of me from high school and wanted nothing to do with me. I was that cocky, arrogant jock from high school who was full of himself. And she was all set with that!

When I walked in to the branch I recognized her from high school. Later that same night I walked in to her part-time job, where she worked in a men's clothing store in one of the local malls. My dad and I were going to watch a Clint Eastwood movie in the cinema, and we had some time to spare before the movie, so we walked into the retail store next door, which happened to be Michele's store. As I saw her there I walked over to her, and we started to talk. I asked her if she went to Central High School, and she said yes. We quickly established who our circle of friends were from high school. We talked about college, and I asked her what her plans were. She told me she was thinking of going to Rhema College.

At this point I had been a Christian for four years. When she told me that I immediately knew she was a Christian. So I asked her if she was a Christian, and she said yes. Of course, being the practical joker that I am, I asked her a few more questions and probably made her feel a little uncomfortable about the conversation. I never even told her that I was a Christian at that time. The movie was about to start, so I said good-bye. After I left a couple of coworkers knew me from church and told her I was a Christian and attended the same church she did. Michele was totally floored; she thought to herself that there was no way this guy could be a Christian.

Shortly thereafter we became friendly and would talk at church periodically. One night Michele and I had gone out to Friendly's for an ice cream purely as friends. As I was driving her home I drove by my old brown house and pointed to it and told her that that's where I grew up. She about fell out of the car! She swung her head and said to me, "You are the boy Steve from the brown house! You and I roller-skated together when I was ten years old at Happy Wheels. We skated together on the 'couples skate' to a song by Foreigner, 'I was waiting for a girl like you.'"

I sat there stunned, trying to make sense of and recollect what she had just said to me. As I thought about it and she kept talking, I remembered roller-skating with a girl when I was twelve years old. This girl had a sweater with a big ice cream cone on the front and a big comb sticking out of her jean back pocket. We only skated to one song because she was shy and hid in the bathroom for just about the rest of the day. After all, she was ten.

A few months later after that night Michele and I went to a New Year's Eve event together in 1992. This was the night that we kissed for the first time. For the record, Michele kissed me! The moment we kissed, I knew I would marry her.

Little did I know that the Lord had already spoken to Michele about six months earlier regarding her husband. While getting ready in the morning one day the Lord spoke to her and told her, "You will meet your husband today." That was the day that I walked into the bank to get a car loan. When I walked in the Lord said to her, "That's him." She had no clue I was a Christian. When the Lord said that to her, she thought, "Dear Lord, not him!"

We have been married since 1993 and have an amazing marriage. I would say we are one-percenters when it comes to our marriage. However, Michele's and my decisions had everything to do with being in the plan of God for our lives. Michele was the woman that God hand-picked for me, and I for her. When you start dating people you're not suppose to be with, things can get turned sideways in a hurry. God had a plan for us, and God has a plan for you. From before we were born God had Michele and I hand-picked to be married, the very best of what He had to offer to us. When you do it God's way, it truly can be that good.

Chapter Six

DRAWING THE LINE

SINCE THE DAY Michele and I got married, we wanted to get closer to God and continue to learn how to walk by faith. We read books, listened to teachings, and genuinely worked at improving a little bit each day. We read from people such as Kenneth Copeland, Creflo Dollar, Fred Price, and Jesse Duplantis. We were having a great time of growing and learning from the Lord.

For over a period of ten plus years, we really grew as Christians. During this season in our lives we were standing on the Word of God for His promises to come to pass. We were learning how faith worked so we would find the Word of God on the topic, and we would declare and decree His Word. When the prosperity message came out, we were all over it. We knew it was right; we sought it out in the Word for ourselves and would declare, "We are the rich." If we heard revelation or instruction by a minister that we trusted and we saw it in the Word, we tried to take hold of it and implement it in our lives. What were we doing during this time? We were getting the Word in us. We were meditating on the Word and talking about the Word to change our thinking to line up with the Word. We were doing our best to be good students and good disciples.

These were years of growth, change, and maturing. But then there came a point in our lives where we realized something was not working right. I was declaring and decreeing the Word, but I kept making missteps. I was very much in the student mode of learning, which is not a bad thing. However, if someone that I respected suggested I should pursue something financially, I would not think twice about it and jump all over it, and that was a problem. Just because it's a God thing for someone else does not mean it's a God thing for me.

At the time, I believed God to be a vice president in the company I was in. I was also looking at ways to buy real estate, and if I even got a sniff of a way to be rich I would jump right in. Someone that I totally respected felt I should be doing a particular business venture, so I pursued it. Another friend of mine that was already very wealthy started talking to me about the stock market, so I jumped in on that too.

This went on for a period of about five years. One day my wife looked at me, frustrated with where we were at, and said she was done doing this. Although I was frustrated with our situation, I kind of looked at her like a deer in headlights. I just did not see what was really going on in our lives. Michele had put her foot down and drew the line in the sand and said no more. It kind of surprised me, but honestly I was on a roller coaster ride and did not know how to get off, and I knew it. I'm glad someone pulled the lever and stopped the ride. Over the next month we stopped everything and started talking things through. We were in a funk, and we were trying to figure out why and how we got here.

When the roller coaster ride stopped we found ourselves thirty-five thousand dollars in credit card debt. How could that be? On the surface we were doing all the right faith-based things. We were believing, declaring, tithing, sowing, and doing what we saw in the Word. Yet we were totally frustrated, going deeper into debt and anxious all the time.

As we started to evaluate the situation and take an inventory of our lives, one of the first questions we asked had to do with this side business we had started. Why were we doing this business venture? As we stopped to think about it, it was because someone that we totally loved, respected, and trusted told us he felt like we should do it. Why were we investing in the stock market? It was because another wealthy friend was giving us good information and helping us do it. Why were we investing in the foreign exchange market? It was because that same friend turned us on to that as well.

Can you see the common theme here? We started to realize that although these people are wonderful, well-respected Christian leaders, they were not the Lord. What was the problem? The problem was we were super quick to just listen to good Christian people and began laboring to build a house without asking the Lord if this was the house He wanted built.

Big revelation number one was that although the Word of God declares we are the rich, it's not my job to go make that happen. It's not your job either.

Big revelation number two was that I was taking the Word of God and trying to force situations I created to work to my benefit with the Word of God. What had we been doing? We were going out on our own and striving to make things in the Word happen for us. As a result we were anxious, frustrated, and in the hole financially.

As we took the time to talk and pray this through, Michele and I realized what had happened. We went before the Lord and repented for going our own way and doing our own thing under the masquerade of the Word. Although we did not realize it, we were trying to *fulfill His Word* by using *our plans*. That will not work. We repented, received our forgiveness, and took communion with the Lord.

We drew the line in the sand. No more. We will never do that again.

What line did we draw? We made the decision that unless the Holy Spirit told us or initiated it in us to do something, we were not doing it. Period. End of story. It didn't matter who spoke to us. We will hear it and take it to the Lord. If the Lord tells us to do it, we do it. If the Lord doesn't, we leave it alone.

Let me point this in perspective for you. If you have children, the goal is to raise them to be godly, of course, but you are also raising them to be self-sufficient adults that can live a successful life without you. You want them to grow up and mature and make good life decisions. Well, isn't that what the scriptures teach us about maturing in the Lord? For Michele and I, we had diligently developed in our relationship with the Lord, with the Holy Spirit and with the Word. We knew the Lord's voice. We just weren't taking the time to listen. In the absence of listening to His voice, there are many other voices, many of them good and well-meaning, that will tell you or suggest to you what you should do. The goal in your Christian walk is to mature to a point where you can hear the Lord for yourself.

Romans 8:14 is one of my favorite scriptures that reminds us that He is leading us: "For as many as are led by the Spirit of God, they are the Sons of God." Just so we are clear, I am not above anyone. We absolutely live in line and follow the Word of God. However, when it comes to any decisions or initiatives beyond what I will call basic living in line with the Word of God, I will not move unless I have heard the Holy Spirit instruct me to do so.

During this time of listening to other well-meaning Christians, we had accumulated credit card debt of over thirty-five thousand dollars. After we drew the line in the sand and made things right with the Lord, we asked Him and believed Him to help us get out of debt. Within six months, our debt of thirty-five thousand dollars was totally paid off. Amazing! To be honest, we still don't know exactly how that happened, but it did.

Once we drew the line in the sand, it seemed like everything in our life shifted. We were no longer chasing, we were no longer striving, we were no longer trying to force things with the Word. In a very short amount of time, the storm and commotion totally settled down, and the peace of God moved in. For the first time in many years it was calm waters and blue skies. Life became much simpler.

We had gone through a season of major growth and maturity in the Word. I think because of my personality I would take what I had learned and would implement the faith side of it with the Word, but I would use my plans to try and make it happen. Other than taking my own initiatives (my plans), everything else I was doing was totally in line with the Word and right. It was not wrong; it was just *incomplete*. It's like ordering a peanut butter and jelly sandwich, taking a bite into it, and only tasting the peanut butter. The tithing, sowing, believing, declaring, and decreeing is absolutely right. However, if in a vacuum by itself, it is incomplete. You must add to it the jelly! What is the jelly? The jelly is understanding that God already has a plan prearranged for you to walk in, and you must follow the leading of the Holy Spirit to walk in it.

Tithing is a no brainer. We have a covenant with God; many call it the covenant of exchange. When you obey Him in the tithe, you get the blessing (Mal. 3:10). It's just that simple. When you get the blessing and learn to operate with the blessing, man, life is so good! Proverbs 10:22 says, "The blessing of the LORD, it maketh rich, and he addeth no sorrow [or toil]." No one can talk me out of the tithe and the blessing, no one. You bring the tithe to Him; He brings the blessing to you. This is a no brainer to me.

However, what I was doing was trying to force the Word to come to pass and then initiate my plan or someone else's plan that I thought sounded good to make the Word happen in my life. Do you see how subtle that is? From the outside looking in, everything looked right and sounded right. From a biblical faith perspective, I was tithing and standing on the Word, but it was not working. I will *never* do that again. It flat out just won't work. *His power* comes with *His plan*, not yours. Find out what His plan is for your life, for your situation, and then believe Him for it.

Now I follow the Word of God, and I allow the Holy Spirit to initiate His plan. When He does, I ask Him for the wisdom on it. The Lord will then bring me to a specific word (we call it the *rhema* Word). The *rhema*

Word is the key that opens and brings the promise to me. I follow the Holy Spirit in how to use the *rhema* Word He gives me.

Can you see the difference? There is no striving, there is no forcing, there is just listening, inquiring, doing, and receiving. Let me spell that out for you:

- Listen to the Holy Spirit.

- Inquire on the how-to.

- Do what He shows you to do.

- Receive the promise.

When Michele and I figured this out, everything shifted into place for us. I found myself going back to Romans 8:14 often: "As many as are led by the Spirit of God, they are the sons of God." In addition to a couple of specific verses, I also found myself continually referring back to two books by Kenneth E. Hagin called *Plans, Purposes, and Pursuits* and *How You Can Be Led by the Spirit of God*. We'll talk more about that later. These two books have had a major impact on my life.

If you find yourself frustrated today, there is a good chance you are trying to go about things on your own. Stop everything you are doing. Go to God and ask Him what's going on, and stay quiet long enough until you hear Him. He will tell you. Once He does, don't run off. Ask Him what He would have you do and then do that for the rest of your life.

The remaining chapters you are about to read have to do with the sub-title of this book, *A Handbook for Fulfilling the Call of God for Your Life*. The Lord has given me pictures, images, and concepts to share to help explain how things work in His Kingdom and how to be massively effective in the call God He has placed on every person. Some of these concepts will be totally new to you, but I urge you to ask the Lord to reveal these things to you.

Chapter Seven

GUARDRAILS

Webster's Dictionary Online describes guardrails as "a system designed to keep people or vehicles from (in most cases unintentionally) straying into dangerous or off-limits areas."[1] The purpose of a guardrail is to keep you safe. Why? Because there are dangerous or off-limit areas that could bring harm or death. When I think of a guardrail I think of how they have been strategically placed so as to keep me and my car on the road and not in a ditch, up a tree, or worse, off a cliff. Naturally speaking, guardrails are extremely important. We have put them all over the roads and highways of our country. Guardrails have saved thousands of lives.

In the same manner that we have physical guardrails to help keep us on the road while driving, did you know you can have spiritual guardrails in place for your spiritual life? We know how important they are naturally, but how much more important should they be spiritually? Several years ago I put up my spiritual guardrails for my life. These guardrails are all based on the Word of God and have had a serious impact on the quality of my life. Once I established these guardrails, they helped me to stay in the center of the road for the will of God for my life. They have also prevented me from veering off the road and getting into a car wreck.

This whole notion of guardrails evolved and came into being over several years for me. Why did the Lord reveal this to me? It's very simple: I was all over the road. Let me explain what I mean. My natural personality makeup is one that likes new things. I have a natural tendency to go after the shiny new toy. Because of that fact, I have made many mistakes and have chased many things that I should have never gone after along the way. What would happen? An idea to go do something or have something would pop into my head, and of course I would want to go do it. Would I pray about it? Of course I would—while I'm running on my way to doing it! I'd say a quick prayer like, "Lord, bless this!" and then I'd be off and running. I'm sure I'm the only one that's ever done this. All I can say is,

it's a good thing my wife loves me the way she does! I have definitely frustrated her along the way.

This natural tendency has caused me to veer off the road many, many
times. And when you veer off the road, you hit trees, you fall in ditches—
you take a beating. I sought the Lord on how to remedy this in my life.
Over a period of many years of praying, reading, and seeking, He has
shown me how to create guardrails, which are areas of discipline that have
kept me in the center of the will of God for my life. Through this process
of identifying what is truly important, I have also simplified my walk with
the Lord, and that has been a wonderful thing.

So let me begin with my concept of guardrails. It begins with one's
desire to want to follow the Lord and stay in the middle of the road as it
relates to the will of God. I take time on a regular basis to read and meditate the Word of God. However, there are three main areas that I focus on
to make sure that I'm in a good place in these areas as it relates to my relationship with the Lord. These three things keep me in the middle of the
road as it relates to the plan of God for my life.

- Walk in love

- Believe God

- Follow the leading of His Spirit

Some may say that it's not that simple and there are so many more
things that we as Christians must be upholding and doing. You can say
what you want; I have been a diligent student over twenty years, and when
I keep these three things top priority in my life, I'm in the zone when it
comes to my walk with the Lord and fulfilling His plan. You can com-
plicate your Christian walk if you want, but serving the Lord is not hard.
People make it hard. The Lord has made it easy.

WALK IN LOVE: MARK 12:30–31, JOHN 13:34

This is the first and second commandment, to love God with all of your
heart, mind, soul and strength and then to walk in love with everyone
else. Jesus gave us a new commandment in John 13:34, "That ye love one
another; as I have loved you, that ye also love one another."

My first goal in life is to live a life that is close and connected with the
Lord. That means having my heart close to His and being aware of His

presence in my life. Walking in love with others was more difficult at first for me. I really had to spend time in the Word to expand my love walk in this area. In Romans 5:5, it says, "The love of God is shed abroad in our hearts by the Holy Ghost which is given unto us." I have spent much time meditating on this verse in order to expand my capacity to walk in love with other people.

The primary reason we want to walk in love is because we belong to the Lord and He is love, and we represent Him to other people. People should be able to see a huge difference in us by our love walk. The secondary reason is that your faith will not work without a solid love walk. I've heard it said many times that your faith acts as the tires on the car, but your love walk is the air in the tires. I've also heard it said that your faith is the curtain, and your love walk is the curtain rod. In both cases, your faith will not work if your love walk is not intact. I will not allow myself to get offended, because in the end it will only hurt me. I cannot allow the blessing of God on my life to get short-circuited. It is way, way, way too valuable to me.

BELIEVE GOD: HEBREWS 11:6

Believing God means to have faith in His Word. It means to spend time in His Word and to meditate on it. As you meditate on the Word, your capacity to believe (which is your faith) is expanded. If my mind doesn't agree with or challenges the Word of God, I must spend more time in His Word to allow the Holy Spirit to bring the revelation of it to me and in me. Believe His Word above all else, even if it seems not to line up with your current reality. That's the cool thing about the Word: it is the final authority and has within it the ability to change natural circumstances.

FOLLOW THE LEADING OF HIS SPIRIT: ROMANS 8:14

The third area I focus on is being led by the Holy Spirit. Romans 8:14 says, "For as many as are led by the Spirit of God, they are the sons of God." This is one of my favorite verses in the whole Bible because it reminds me who is leading me in the fulfillment of the call of God on my life. Remember, I was the guy that when an idea popped in my head, I would want to go do it. Because of that, I was all over the road, and many times in a ditch, all the while taking my wife along with me. Yikes! If you develop a lifestyle of listening to the Holy Spirit and following Him as He leads, then He will lead you right into the plan of God for your life.

I will come back to guardrails in a minute, as I want to go deeper as it relates to being led by the Holy Spirit. My problem was that I had thoughts popping into my head, and for the most part I would run off and chase them. I was not able to discern right thoughts from wrong thoughts. So let's take a few minutes and let me share with you what the Lord has shown me about thoughts, because it has everything to do with following the leading of the Holy Spirit.

As far as I can tell, thoughts come from five primary areas. You may find more, and that's fine, but I think I have the major categories covered. If you will take the time to understand this, it will help you to stop wasting time and energy.

The five primary areas thoughts come from are:

- Natural thinking
- The media
- Other people
- The enemy
- The Holy Spirit

The majority of your thoughts do not come from the Holy Spirit. As you begin to understand this and spend more time in His Word, you can train yourself to quickly discern when the Holy Spirit initiates a thought in you, versus the many other thoughts that come from different sources.

The next thing you need to know is that you can take authority over all thoughts and kick out the ones that do not belong there. As a matter of fact, that is part of your job. Second Corinthians 10:5 says, "Casting down imaginations, and every high thing that exalteth itself against the knowledge of God, and *bringing into captivity every thought* to the obedience of Christ" (emphasis added). Keep your heart and thought life close to Him. Discern which thoughts do not come from Him, and remove them from your thinking. Know when the Holy Spirit is initiating something in you, and then follow only that.

Look at the image below. I believe it will help you tremendously. The goal is to discipline yourself to only do what the Holy Spirit prompts and leads you to do.

I live my life by three primary principles: walk in love, believe God, and follow His leading. This keeps me in the center of the road. However, we all know that there are forks in the road, many exits and turns, or just plain getting stuck in the ditch. This is why spiritual guardrails are so important.

Previously I have referenced two books by Kenneth E. Hagin that have been keys to my walk with the Lord, *How You Can Be Led by the Spirit of God* and *Plans, Purposes, and Pursuits*. These are the books the Lord has shown me to use as my left and right guardrails. For the past several years, every time I have needed to make an important decision I have gone back and reread the highlights of these two books. I have used them as my spiritual guardrails. They have become a checklist for me to make sure that I don't veer off the road and I stay in the center of the will of God for my life. I made the decision that I was all done making mistakes and wasting valuable time. So every time I have a decision to make, I reread the highlights of these books, and I am happy to report that I have stayed in the center of His will.

So here are my spiritual guardrails. My left guardrail comes from the book *How You Can Be Led by the Spirit of God*. I have taken the highlights from this book and have simplified them in checklist format for you to follow. When I need to make an important decision, I go to my guardrails, and I carefully review each question and make sure I answer it honestly before the Lord.

Left Guardrail

1. Who initiated it? What is the origin of this thought or idea? Natural me? Someone else? The media? The enemy? The Holy Spirit? Page 87

2. Praying in the Spirit, seeking Him and getting quiet. Answers are within. Page 11–12, 25–27.

3. What is a no? Page 24 What is a yes? Page 25

4. Practice the Word. Am I in line with the Word of God?[2] Page 126

Once I go through my left guardrail, I come over to my right guardrail, which comes from the book *Plans, Purposes, and Pursuits*. I review each question carefully, one at a time. I give it thought and go to the Lord with it and inquire of Him.

Right Guardrail

1. Whatever you are doing, ask God, "Is this your plan?" Page 9
   If you have the wrong plan it will definitely fail.
   If you add to His plan it won't work.

2. Don't be too busy to find out. You can go your whole life and miss the plan of God. Page 29

3. Timing: Wait for the quickening of the Holy Spirit. Page 38

4. Just being sensitive? Vs. For me to do? Seek Him for the plan. Page 38–41
   • If no plan is given, it's not for you to do.
   • If the how-to plan is given, it's for you to do.
   • If a plan is given, seek Him for the purpose and timing.[3]

Always, always, always remember this: if God isn't in it, you don't want it.

Let me tell you something. There is some work involved on your part. Your work is to take the time and go before the Lord. Do you have to do this every time? Nope! However, you don't have to succeed every time either! I have made the decision that I am all done wasting time, energy, and resources. I have learned that if I will take the time to go through this process when I need to make a decision, these guardrails or questions will keep me in the center of the road, in the center of the will of God for my life.

Doing this doesn't mean you will never miss it again. But here's what it will do for you. It will dramatically increase your success rate with the Lord. Isn't that why you're reading this book? I know it is.

I have put all of this together in a picture to help you. The details of the guardrails are above, but this is a good visual to refer back to often throughout your life. I hope you refer to it every time you need to make a decision.

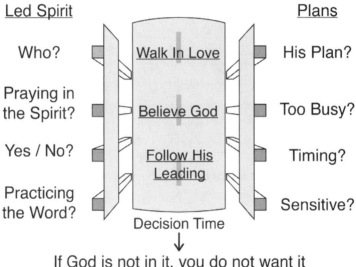

Led Spirit   Plans

Who?   Walk In Love   His Plan?

Praying in
the Spirit?   Believe God   Too Busy?

Yes / No?   Follow His   Timing?
                        Leading

Practicing
the Word?   Sensitive?

                        Decision Time
                             ↓
        If God is not in it, you do not want it

Chapter Eight

DOMINOES

I N ORDER FOR me to discuss the concept of dominoes, I need to lay a foundation in the Word. Ephesians 2:10 says, "For we are his workmanship, created in Christ Jesus unto good works, which *God hath before ordained that we should walk in them*" (emphasis added). I also really like the Amplified Bible version of this verse, which says, "For we are God's [own] handiwork (His workmanship), recreated in Christ Jesus, [born anew] that we may do those good works which God predestined (*planned beforehand*) for us [*taking paths which He prepared ahead of time*], that we should walk in them [living the good life which *He prearranged* and made ready for us to live]" (emphasis added).

You come to earth preprogrammed. God Himself created you! He then strategically and carefully hand delivered you to the earth and placed inside of you blueprints for your life. These blueprints explain how you are wired, explain how you are supposed to function and lay out all the things He has created for you to accomplish and to be.

It is a step-by-step manual on how you work, what makes you tick, and what you are created for in this life. It explains how there is only one of you in the earth, that you are massively important to His plan in the earth, and only *you* can do what you were created to do. It explains to follow the blueprint for your life carefully, and if you do, you can function to the fullest, in the capacity you were created for.

I use this blueprint analogy all the time because it is helpful in understanding your relationship and walk with the Lord. God had a plan for you before you were ever born. It far surpasses anything you could ever conceive or do on your own. So you have a choice; you can either do your own thing or you can pursue the plan of God for your life. If your desire is to fulfill the plan of God for your life, then you need to understand the concept of your life having blueprints.

Generally speaking, the purpose of a blueprint is to build something. That something doesn't exist yet; it is an image in someone's mind. Blueprints take this image in someone's mind and put structure around it, a plan for bringing this image into being. That's what God did when He created you. Jeremiah tells us, "Before I formed thee in the belly I knew thee" (Jer. 1:5).

OK, so the Lord knew you. He had an image of you in His mind before He created you. But how far back? Ephesians 1:4 tells us, "According as he hath chosen us in him before the foundation of the world…" Before the Lord created the foundation of the world, He knew you, He chose you, and He created you with His very own hands. After all, Ephesians 2:10 tells us "we are *his* workmanship" (emphasis added). When He created you, He also created your blueprint, your future, your life's plan and life's work. That's why Psalm 37:23 says, "The steps of a good man are ordered by the LORD." He pre-planned *every step* of your life before you were ever born!

I am not talking about predestination in the sense that God has already chosen who is going to be saved and who is not. Let me frame this up very simply: Man has a free will, and he can choose to believe in God or not. Although God has created an amazing plan for everyone, it is up to the individual whether or not he or she is going to believe in the Lord. If they believe in the Lord, it is still a daily choice on whether to serve Him and follow His leading for that day. It is a choice that we make knowingly or unknowingly every day.

Let me make this crystal clear. Everyone has a God-given destiny and calling for their life—whether you walk in it or not is up to the decisions you make. If you choose to make your own decisions, then you are responsible for how your life turns out. Or you can choose God's destiny and design for your life, a life that many only dream about.

If you can understand that God has preplanned and prearranged every step of your life in a sequence of events, then you will be able to understand the concept of dominoes. Have you ever watched one of those domino championship competitions? You see a team of people constructing and creating an amazing sequence of events with dominoes. The first thing they do that you normally do not see is they think about, plan, and create in their minds what they want to build. Once everything has been planned out and created in their minds or on paper, then they go build that image. Once it is built, they sit back and take in their masterpiece.

Then the competition begins. At the appointed time, one of the team members touches the first domino and begins the chain of events. Once the first domino goes down, it touches the next domino and so on until eventually all of the dominoes go down. Whether you are young or old, everyone loves to watch this amazing display!

I want you to think of your life like an amazing display of dominoes. Each domino is a preplanned event in your life that God has put there for you to walk in and be blessed by. These dominoes are only found in a predetermined path that God has already orchestrated for you to walk in. Each domino is connected to the next domino in some way. When you are in the plan of God following the leading of the Holy Spirit, you can walk right into the next domino. These dominoes are dominoes of blessing and goodness, and God has placed them there to enrich your life.

The issue is a matter of trust, however. If you truly know the Lord intimately, you will trust Him that He has your entire life already orchestrated in a beautiful display. What happens if one domino does not go in the correct direction? Everything stops. It does not advance any further. This is what happens when we choose to make our own decision and go in our own direction. We disconnect ourselves from the plan of God that He has already orchestrated for us and start to take our own steps, making our own paths, rather than following the steps that are ordered by the Lord.

This is the issue for most Christians. They love the Lord, but they chose to take their own steps and make their own decisions. Basically, they pick up the blueprint for their life, look at it, and then drop it to the ground behind them and just start taking steps in the direction that seems right to them. Many of them are walking around aimlessly with no direction and no understanding of the bigger picture of what God has planned for them and called them to. It's like the lab experiments with mice and cheese. The mouse continues to go down dead ends, and it has to turn around and try yet another path to get to the cheese. Proverbs 14:12 applies to these people. It says, "There is a way which seemeth right unto a man, but the end thereof are the ways of death."

Wouldn't it be a whole lot easier to just follow the Lord step-by-step and never make a bad turn, take a bad path, or make a wrong decision? If you continue to find yourself in dead end situations, there is hope for you! God has never and will never change the plan He has for you! No matter how many times you've missed it, there is mercy and grace for you! His mercies are new every morning, and His plans don't change. Romans 11:29 says "For the gifts and *calling* of God are without repentance" (emphasis added). I will say it again: God will not and has never changed His plan and His calling for your life.

No matter where you find yourself right now, you can get reconnected with the plan of God for your life. It begins with repenting, asking for forgiveness, and then taking the time to ask Him what His next step is for your life *and* staying quiet before Him long enough to know what He's telling you. He will lead you to that next step, that next domino in your life. For many Christians, this will be a new concept or way of living. This is a different way of living, and it will require you to work at it. This book will take you step by step on how to reengineer your thinking so you can live this way.

I would like to highlight one area for a moment that is critical to successful Christian living and listening to the direction of the Holy Spirit. A big mistake I see many Christians make is thinking they can chose to go to any church they want to. They attend a church for a while, serving in different capacities. But somewhere along the line they get offended at something that was said or done, and they allow an offense to move them out and into another church.

Jesus is the Head of the church and places people in churches as *He wills*, not as you will. That's why 1 Corinthians 12:18 says, "But now hath God set the members every one of them in the body, as it hath pleased him." If the Lord brought you to a church, then learn to not take offense, and stay where Jesus placed you. If you left a pastor that God brought you to because of an offense, repent, make it right with the Lord and your pastor and go back. If the pastor is not preaching the Word of God, is in sin, or is abusive, you can leave. Other than that, stay and bloom where you are planted. *You being in the right church that the Lord has called you to is critical to the plan of God in your life.* The plan of God for your life will not work right if this is wrong.

Once we have the pastor and church right, if we stay close to Jesus we will have a general sense of the direction and calling God has for us. At times we will even see glimpses down the road of the domino path for our life. Because this is a new concept for many, take the time and really mediate on the picture below. While you are doing that, think about your life and ask the Holy Spirit to begin to reveal this to you. Don't be so quick to rush off of this page. Slow down and allow the Holy Spirit the opportunity to show you and direct you. Yes, this is probably a different way to operate than you're used to, but give it some time and let God begin to show you.

This first picture shows our day-to-day living and decisions that are made. Although your life is an amazing display of dominoes orchestrated by the Lord Himself, most of the time you will only see the immediate domino that is right in front of you. After you have taken the time to ask the Lord to reveal this to you, you will know that there is a whole chain or connection of dominoes for your life. However, right now, you have a decision to make, and you have one domino in front of you. You can either choose to trust the Lord and follow the leading of the Holy Spirit into this next domino, or you can make your own decision and go the way that seems right to you.

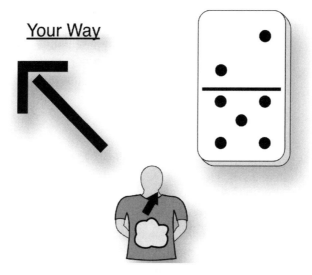

The second picture is a reminder to you that your life has already been *completely* preplanned. The Lord created an amazing chain of events, places, people, blessings, and goodness for you. If you'll stay close to Him and pay attention to Him, He will prepare you before the next turn in the road.

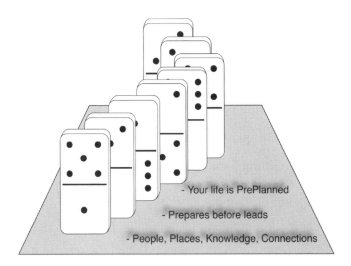

- Your life is PrePlanned
- Prepares before leads
- People, Places, Knowledge, Connections

It's very easy for us to forget that God put this domino here for us and that if we follow the leading of the Holy Spirit, He will walk us right into the plan and goodness of God. We can also forget that there is a chain, a string, or a path of dominoes behind this one and that they are all connected, that your life is connected.

So what do we do? We choose to make our own decisions because we think we know better, and we go do our own thing and stop the domino chain. Once we do that, we are on our own, making our own way and providing our own needs. We have moved out of the grace of God and moved into the mercy of God.

Thank God for His mercy, but living in the mercy of God is not like living in the grace of God. The grace of God is in His perfect will, living in the dominoes that He prearranged for us. Life is good! Although there may be a few bumps in the road, the road has already been cleared and prepared for you! All of the provisions that you will ever need are already lined up and waiting for you!

The mercy of God is when you are on your own path, making your own way. You have limited the Lord's involvement in your life. There are no preplanned provisions in the path for you; you are kind of on your own with limited coverage from the Lord. If the rain comes, you have removed yourself from the Lord's path, and you *will* get wet.

Psalm 37:23 read, "The steps of a good man are ordered by the LORD." Another way to say it would be, "The dominoes of a man have been planned, orchestrated, and designed by the Lord Himself".

Trust in the Lord that He already put an amazing plan in place for you to walk in. It's far, far better than anything you could ever do. He put His Holy Spirit in you to lead you to the next domino so you would never miss out on anything and would always walk in the best that God has for you. Stay in the dominoes; your life will become an amazing display of the goodness of God!

Chapter Nine

THE MOUNTAIN OF GOD

T O THINK ABOUT the fact that God planned out your entire life before you were ever born is nothing short of awesome. It shows that you were not a mistake, you were not an after thought, that God sits out of time and had you in the forefront of His mind! He planned out your entire life because He is totally head-over-heels in love with you! You are the reason He died on the cross, to redeem you out of sin and put you on His team with His plan and His power to fulfill it! That's pretty heavy duty stuff—but it's true.

Whether you got saved when you were young, middle-aged, or older, that's when you became part of His team, and that's when your journey with Him began. Since God is not boring, neither are His plans for you. He created a life for you that is chock *full* of adventure and fulfillment in every area of your life. As you walk with the Lord, think of your life as a journey, a journey where you climb the mountain of God. Your mission in life, should you choose to accept it, is to climb the mountain of God.

What is the mountain of God? It is the plan of God for your life. His plan has a path and steps that He has predetermined and preestablished for you to walk in from before you were even born. I'm going to lay a couple of concepts and images in place for you to truly comprehend what the mountain of God is for your life.

The first thing I want you to think about and imagine is the last time you were in an airplane. Have you ever taken off at an airport where you were near a wooded or forested area? When you looked down at the wooded area, did you see *power lines* that cut right through the wooded area? Maybe you saw a forest with trees everywhere and then all of a sudden there was a very clear, straight, and distinct path that had been fully cleared out. This path is the power line path and goes from one destination clear across to another destination. There are no trees, holes, or big boulders in the path. By the time those lines are active, that path has already been cleared out, and an infrastructure has been put in that path in order to run power through it.

I want you to think about this path because this is the picture of the plan of God for your life. It's a predetermined path that has already been cleared for you. There are no trees to cut down. There are no bridges to build, and you could walk or ride a four-wheeler through this path with relative ease. Not only has He cleared the way for you, but He put His power and protection in this path for you. If your desire is to follow the Lord, this is where it's at for your life. The blessing of God, the protection of God, and the grace of God are working at optimal performance in this place.

Most people don't understand this, and that's why they veer off the path and start cutting down their own trees to make their own way. When you get into the woods, you are on your own. You are creating your own way. It is by the sweat of your brow and the toil of your hands. You have made the decision to provide for yourself.

God's power and protection is just as strong as it ever was; it's just that you moved away from it. When you take your own path, there is limited help or power from the Lord on your path, just mercy. You are standing in the rain with no umbrella over your life. This place is called the mercy of God. It's when you venture out on your own and you eventually figure out that it's not the place that God has predetermined for you, and you get on your knees and eventually repent and cry out for the mercy of God. Thank God His mercies are new every morning! That means you can repent any time, and He'll forgive you and take you back in an instant.

But why would you live your life in the woods cutting down trees and providing for yourself when the Lord has already made a path clear for you and has provided His power, provision, and protection for you? What's easier: driving a four-wheeler under the power lines or taking the four-wheeler into the woods with no path?

There was a critical point in my life when I trusted the leading of the Holy Spirit. In the natural it was really scary because it was one on of those critical decisions or turns in the road that could be devastating financially if I made the wrong decision. During that time I listened to the *Believer's Voice of Victory* (BVOV) series with Kenneth Copeland and Bill Winston from February 2010 over and over and over again. I listened intently to those conversations. Every time I put it on I made the decision I would listen like my life depended on it, like it was the first time I had ever heard it. These BVOV conversations helped to keep me on the path I knew the Holy Spirit had led me to.

If you are not diligent about it, it's very easy to start by following the Holy Spirit and then take control of the wheel and start calling your own shots. I learned *many* things from these conversations, but one particular story that Bill Winston talked about had a dramatic impact on my thought process and understanding.[1]

Bill Winston told a story about a man he knew who said he was going to have all these different types of businesses and that these businesses were going to bring in all kinds of money. He said the money from these businesses would then free him up to be able to minister full-time. He had it all planned out and worked his plan for many, many years. All these years later, even though it sounded like a very good plan, a well-intended plan, a plan that many Christians would think was honorable, his plans never came together and worked for him. Why? Because they were *his plans*; they were man's plans. You can't fulfill God's work with your plans. It just doesn't work.

Bill Winston, however, obeyed God. He was *led by the Holy Spirit* to quit his job and go to Bible school. He obeyed. Did it make sense for him to leave a very good job with a great future and career with a really big company? No. But as he sought the Lord, he knew that he knew this was the plan of God for his life. Then one day, he was prompted by the Holy Spirit to take action. Both he and his wife knew it, so they followed the leading of the Holy Spirit and obeyed what they knew, which was to sell their house and move to Bible school.

The story continued, and Dr. Winston talked about how he followed the Lord one step at a time, or as I like to call it, one domino at a time. Whose plan was Dr. Winston following? The Lord's predetermined plan. Did he know that eventually there would be a domino in his life called a mall? No. But as he followed the leading of the Holy Spirit, the Lord led him to buy an entire mall. The mall and many other blessings were planned events in his future, but Dr. Winston had to follow the leading of the Holy Spirit to walk into them and inherit them. As Dr. Winston believed God and obeyed what he knew to be true, God had higher thoughts, higher plans, and higher ways for him.

This is a great example of two believers, both who loved God and wanted in their hearts to serve Him. One man made his own decisions and chose to cut down his own trees and make his own path. He never inquired of the Lord as to the Lord's plan and path for his life. As a result, he has labored but all in vain because it's not what the Lord called him to do.

> Except the LORD build the house, they labour in vain that build it.
> —PSALM 127:1

The other man, Dr. Winston, sought the Lord, and although it didn't make sense in the natural to leave a really good job to go to Bible school, he chose the Lord's plan. In the Lord's plan, a few dominoes down the road, the Lord had a domino called a mall and then another domino called a bank in his future. The Lord eventually brought Brother Winston into owning a mall and a bank (and probably much more that I don't know about). The point is, God already has your life planned out and has great things in your future! If you trust in Him and follow Him, He'll walk you right into them.

There are many Christians I know (and you too) that always seem to be in the woods. Life seems to always be hard for them, and there is always something wrong. These people are constantly struggling and always in need of prayer. The issue for these people is not that God does not love them but that they have not taken the time to seek the Lord and find out what His plan is for their lives and then begin to follow that. They have made their own decisions. They are in the woods cutting down their own trees and wondering why it's so hard to serve the Lord and be blessed like they read about in the Scriptures. They need to get out of living in the mercy of God and get into living in the grace of God. They need to stop cutting down their own trees and get back on God's path, the plan of God for their life.

Now imagine this power line, in a cleared-out path as it goes up a mountain.

The path is always clear; however, sometimes it turns to the left for a length of time and then continues up the mountain. Sometimes it turns to the right for a period of time and then continues up the mountain. In the plan of God for your life, we need to recognize that there are seasons of *preparation* and seasons of *promotion*. You could also say that there are seasons of *development* and seasons of *advancement*. It is not just promotion and advancement! What good is it to be promoted in an area of your life if you have not developed the necessary skills and character to sustain that promotion?

God will take you through seasons of preparation to develop the things that are necessary for you to be massively successful and not only sustain the promotion but prepare you for the next level up. If you know you are in the will of God, the plan of God, and you are not being promoted, it means you are in a time of preparation. Recognize it for what it is and embrace it. Ask yourself and the Lord to show you the areas that He is trying to develop in you. The sooner you embrace it and allow the Lord to develop you, the sooner you get to graduate and move on to your next level of promotion.

I had two seasons of development in my life that lasted very different time periods and developed different areas. One of my preparation seasons lasted about six years. It was a time of serious growth, learning, and development. Although it wasn't necessarily always fun at the time, I developed and built muscles in areas that became very important in the next phase of promotion. Another season of development in my life lasted about six months, and I got what I needed and was able to move up to the next phase rather quickly.

Many Christians get out of the will of God during times of preparation. They think because they are not getting promoted it must not be the will of God for their life. Big mistake. If you followed the Lord to the place you are currently in, then recognize the season of development that you are in and trust the Lord that He knows what He's doing, because He does.

I want to layer a third concept on top of what we have been discussing. As you think about power lines in a clear-cut path up the mountain of God, I want you to put your dominoes in the power line path. The concept is this: In the plan of God for your life, there are predetermined dominoes in your path for you to walk in. They are events, people, places and divine connections, all with the stamp of the Holy Spirit's anointing on them. When you stay on the path, the dominoes are connected. One domino leads to the next domino, and so on. They are dominoes of blessing, provision, protection, and the goodness of God with the purpose of advancing His Kingdom and enriching your life. When you trust the Lord and follow the leading of the Holy Spirit, He will direct you and lead you right into the next domino. Can you imagine living a life that is blessed and prosperous and the best that God has to offer? You can. It's what He has planned for you all along.

Now, when you put all these concepts of guardrails, dominoes, power lines, and the mountain of God together you get the following picture. Take time to look at and meditate on the picture that God gave me to share with you. God showed me this picture during a Sunday morning worship service at our church.

Below is a list of key terms to look for and understand when reviewing the map.

- **Arrows**: The Holy Spirit directing you into the plan of God (personal GPS)

- **Dominoes**: Dominoes of good that God has preplanned and put into your life

- **Guardrails**: Guardrails to help keep you in the center of the will of God

- **Plan of God**: God's predesigned and perfect plan that He has for you

- **Grace of God**: God's power in you to accomplish His plan (power lines)

- **Development**: Seasons where God is developing and preparing you for your next season of promotion

- **Advancement**: Seasons of promotion from the Lord

- **Traps**: Traps or mirages the enemy will put in your path to make a situation appear naturally enticing and to try and get you out of the will of God

- **Your way**: When you choose what you think is best rather than slowing down to ask Him, or you've asked Him but still don't fully trust Him

- **Trees**: The trees you will have to chop down when you go your own way; you will have to find your own provision and try to be your own protection (i.e., using the world's operating system, which is man's way)

- **Mercy of God**: God trying to protect you from the elements when you're out of the will of God

For some of you, this may be very new. If you find yourself in the woods today because of decisions that you made on your own, you are not in a hopeless situation! If you recently veered off in the woods on your own, God may just bring you back to where you were supposed to be on the path. If you have been walking in the woods for a long time and you think too much time and too many events have gone by and have been missed, I have good news for you too! Although it's not His best, you did not catch God by surprise. Wherever you find yourself right now—you may be deep in the woods, you may have lost out on ten or fifteen years of your life in the woods—it doesn't matter. God has a domino path that He has created for you to *reconnect* you right where you are to the plan of God. Don't lose any more time. Get reconnected with God's plan for your life. He has not changed His mind or calling for you, Romans 11:29 tells us so: "For the gifts and calling of God are without repentance." Start where you are right now and get on with it!

Even when it doesn't make sense to your natural mind, if the Holy Spirit is leading you in a direction (and when it's the Holy Spirit it will always be in line with the Word of God) trust in Him and follow Him into that domino. If you will purpose in your heart to follow the plan of God and to live this way, at the end of your life you will have climbed the mountain of God that *God had planned for you*. Upon that faithful day the Lord will say to you, "Well done, good and faithful servant" (Matt. 25:23).

Chapter Ten

TIMING AND YOUR PERSONAL GPS

I HOPE THAT WHAT I have shared with you thus far regarding the plan of God and the dominoes that God has prearranged in your life have helped you. However, I would be remiss if I did not spend some time talking to you about timing. God has dominoes of blessing and goodness sequentially prearranged and set to happen in particular timeframes. Timing is very important to the plan of God for your life. God has dominoes set to happen in a timeframe in which He has orchestrated connections, people, situations, and provisions for your good.

Simply put, there is timing with God. You can know the plan of God for your life but get out in front of the timing of it and it won't work. In the same manner, you can be driving on the highway and know what city you are going to but still take the wrong exit and get off the highway too early. It's not that you can't get to your destination, but like a navigation system, He has to reroute you through some back roads to get you there. You will make it there, but it may take you a little longer. And you may encounter a few bumps in the road on your way.

As it relates to following the plan of God for your life, the Holy Spirit functions very much like a built-in navigation system. Now please don't get offended. I did not say that the Holy Spirit is a navigation system, because that would grossly under state who the Holy Spirit is (the Spirit of the Most High God, our Father). However, in terms of explaining and describing *how* to follow the *leading* of the Holy Spirit into the plan of God as described in Romans 8:14, 16 and John 16:13, I think this analogy is very fitting and helpful.

If you understand how a navigation system works, you can understand how to follow the leading and guiding of the Holy Spirit for your life. But how is this biblical? When Jesus taught and we read what was recorded in the Bible, we know that Jesus used parables all the time to explain things. Parables are analogies or examples, which is what I'm doing here. He used farming as examples all the time because that's mostly what that generation was doing, and they could understand it. Our generation is the

high-tech generation. By using the right technology as examples, I believe
we can help many people understand how to follow Him more closely and
fulfill the call of God in our lives and establish His Kingdom in the earth.

We all know the basics of how a navigation system works in a car. Let's
do a quick review:

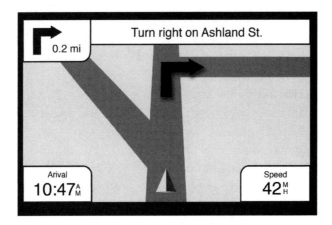

1. A destination is selected.

2. The navigation system (GPS) connects to the satellite in the
   sky, surveys where you are located, and calculates the most
   direct path to lead you to the selected destination.

3. The GPS then provides you with an estimated time of
   arrival (ETA) and sets the course for you to follow to get
   you there.

4. As you begin to move, the GPS communicates with you and
   alerts you of upcoming directional changes.

5. The driver simply follows the arrow on the screen and lis-
   tens to the commands.

Thus far, we have described some of the "how it works." However, there
is the element of time involved in this. There is time involved between
where you are now and where the next turn is. This time is determined by
your ability to stay on course and the rate of your speed.

1. The GPS will not say anything if you're on the right course and if it's not time to turn. You look on the screen and see that you are on track.

2. When you get close to your next turn, the GPS will speak to you and prepare you that your next turn is about to come up. It might say, for example, "In one mile, turn right onto Route 93 South."

3. Just before the turn, the GPS will prompt you again and say, "Turn right onto Route 93 South."

4. If you turn too early or miss your turn, the GPS will recalculate and reroute you back onto the path that leads you to your destination.

5. When you get to your destination, it will tell you, "Arriving at your address."

The Holy Spirit is in you, and He is the Spirit of God your Father in heaven. He knows the plans God has for you, and amongst many other things, He is leading and guiding you into the plan of God for your life.

In the Amplified Bible, John 16:13 reads this way: "But when He, the Spirit of Truth (the Truth-giving Spirit) comes, He will guide you into all the Truth (the whole, full Truth). For He will not speak His own message [on His own authority]; but He will tell whatever He hears [from the Father; He will give the message that has been given to Him], and He will announce and declare to you the things that are to come [that will happen in the future]."

The Holy Spirit is the Spirit of God Himself and was sent to earth by the Father to help you out personally to fulfill the call of God on your life. One of the ways He does that is as your personal navigation system, your personal GPS. He knows where you are suppose to be going and will *navigate you through* and *get you to* where you need to be.

As with any navigation system, there are many paths or turns you can take at any time. This is true in life, and at any time you can choose to take your own turn. When you choose to do this, you shift over to living according to man's ways, or the world's operating system (WOS). When you choose to follow the path that is "lit up in color" with arrows pointing on it, you are choosing God's way, or KOGOS.

I live in New England, and for me, it seems like everything is about an hour away. When I enter the address for my next destination, my navigation system will tell me exactly how to get there and how long it will take to get there. If I listen closely to my navigation system it will prepare me a little bit before my next turn, and then when it's time to turn it will tell me precisely when to turn and where to turn. If I simply follow my navigation system I will reach my destination on time. Thank God for this technology!

This is what it is like when you are following the leading of the Holy Spirit into the plan of God for your life. God already has the most direct route mapped out for you. If you take a wrong turn or get off the highway early, the navigation system, a.k.a. the Holy Spirit, will immediately begin to reroute you back to where you just were. After a short duration, if you do not recognize it and go back to the original route, He will find another route and reroute you to get you back on track, back on course to your destination.

There have been many times in my life when I was following the plan of God, but because of my natural personality I found myself getting off the highway early. I recognized this problem and asked the Lord to help me with it. As He has matured me, I have gone through phases. My first phase of growth was getting the Word of God in me so I would know His Word and trust and depend on His Word. This is where I learned how to live by faith.

The second phase I went through was using my faith with the Word of God but then applying my plans to it. This is the same thing the guy did in the Bill Winston story earlier. Of course, this doesn't work.

The next phase of growth for me was when I figured out that His Word and His anointing only worked with His plan. I made the decision to follow only His plan but sometimes I still got off the highway too early and had to be rerouted.

And now, finally, my fourth stage of growth is where I am now. I seek the Lord for His plan, I stay close to the Holy Spirit and have the patience and discipline to wait for His timing on when to implement His plan.

I'm not saying that I have arrived and have nothing to improve upon! There is always more to learn and more to improve upon. However, I do believe that I have developed to a place where I know how to effectively follow the Lord and have a functional working knowledge of how to walk in the call of God for my life. They are the principles that I have outlined in this book.

I want to make two points very clear to you. First, as you are praying and inquiring, let the Holy Spirit show you and initiate the plan of God in your life. This means that you take the time to quiet down and ask Him what destination He would have you go to. Once you know your next destination, the second point is very similar yet very important: Stay on the course God has you on until the Holy Spirit quickens it in you to make a turn. Just like a navigation system, you will sense that change is on the horizon. That's Him preparing you. That's Him telling you, "Ok, now pay attention because the exit is coming up." The Holy Spirit will then quicken you again shortly thereafter to make the turn and take the exit. If the Holy Spirit has not quickened anything in you, you stay the course and make no changes. It's just not time yet. When the time comes, He will quicken it in you.

Think about how your navigation system works in your car, and you will understand how to follow the leading of the Holy Spirit into the plan of God for your life. You can develop yourself to follow God's route, His preplanned path for your life, and make it to *every destination on time*. If you will do this, you will reach all of the remaining destinations that God already has planned for you, and you will find yourself at the top of the mountain of God at the completion of your life. If you'll follow the Holy Spirit, He will get you to where you're supposed to be going on time and with His power!

Just like following a GPS has to do with location and timing, timing is critical to following the plan of God. In the book *Plans, Purposes, and Pursuits* Kenneth E. Hagin talks all about timing. As a matter of fact, I wrote the word *timing* at the top of the page and underlined it so I could easily go back and reference it when I needed to. Here's what it says:

> Sometimes God will show you what He wants you to do—you will have His plan. But at the same time, you will perceive in your spirit that the *time* to do it isn't quite right. Learn to wait for the right time to implement God's plan—*wait for the quickening of the Holy Spirit*. At other times, God will show you things in the spirit, and although you won't know *everything* God wants to do, as you fulfill what the Lord told you to do— little by little, you will move into deeper areas of the spirit. As

you are obedient to follow God's plan and *His* purpose, He will begin to illustrate and demonstrate some things to you and lead you into greater understanding of His plan.

There will always be times when you simply picked up on what the Spirit wants to do through others in the body of Christ, but that does not mean that God wants *you* to do it.

Listen to what I'm saying. If you'll recall, sometimes when Paul had something to say, he would say, "This is what the Lord said." But at other times, he'd say, "God gave me permission to say this."

Please get something clear in your mind: I'm speaking this by the Spirit of God because God wants to clear up some areas so He can move in our midst. Many people who have some sensitivity to the Holy Spirit sense what God is doing and what He *wants* to do. They [grab] that and run off with it and try to build something from that. But because God didn't specifically tell *them* to do it, their plans are only man's plans, not God's plan or purpose. They add to God's plan or they take away from it, but they get the real thing God wanted to do in a mess, and sometimes they even thwart the plan and the move that God wanted. We can't let that happen in what God wants to do in our day in the body of Christ.[1] (emphasis added)

Here are the things that I have written in the margin of this book as a quick checklist reminder for me personally:

- Timing: Wait for the quickening of the Spirit
- If you do what He has shown you to do, He'll bring you deeper into His plan
- Sensing something does not necessarily mean *you* are supposed to do it
- When God tells me to do something, seek Him on how to do it, the plan. If no plan is given, it's *not* for me to do. It's just me being sensitive.

From reading the chapter on guardrails, you know that this has become part of my guardrail system. It has helped me not to waste time doing things He has not told me to do but rather to focus in on what He has told me to do and follow the quickening of the Holy Spirit when doing it. I went from roaming around in the woods, just chopping down every tree that looked good to me, to following His navigation system that's inside me and beginning to reach God-ordained destinations. I went from missing God most of the time to being dialed into the Holy Spirit and accomplishing things that God gave me to accomplish.

Let me share with you one more explanation and analogy that has really helped me along the way. It comes from the book *Sparkling Gems From the Greek* by Reverend Rick Renner. This is an absolutely amazing book where Rev. Renner takes different topics and expounds on the meaning of the original Greek. In a section called "Is the Holy Spirit 'Tugging' at Your Heart Today?" he talks in detail about Romans 8:14, one of my favorite verses, which says, "As many as are led by the Spirit of God, they are the sons of God." Here is what he writes in this section:

> When your journey of faith begins, you may not have all the answers you would like to have *before* you take your first steps of faith... That's the way it is for all of us when we walk with the Lord. As wonderful as it would be to see the whole picture *before* we get started, He usually leads us one step at a time *after* we get started...
>
> Romans 8:14 says, "as many as are led by the Spirit of God, they are the sons of God." The word "led" is the Greek word *ago*, which described *the act of leading about an animal, such as a cow or a goat, at the end of a rope.* The owner would wrap a rope around the animal's neck and then "tug" and "pull" until the animal started to follow him. When the animal decided to cooperate and follow that gentle tug, it could then be gently "led" to where its owner wanted it to go.
>
> Today I want to encourage you to pay careful attention to the "tugging" and "pulling" of the Holy Spirit in your heart. He is a Gentleman and does not *force* you to obey Him. He prompts you, tugs at your heart, and pulls on your spirit to get your attention. Sometimes His "tugs" may be so gentle that you almost miss them. But if you'll develop your sensitivity to the Holy Spirit, He will gently "lead" you exactly where He wants you to go with your life.

Also, don't demand that the Holy Spirit tell you the whole story first! *Trust Him!* Remember that Jesus called Him the "Spirit of Truth" (John 16:13) to help you understand that the Holy Spirit and His leading can be *trusted!* He is the "Spirit of Truth," so if He is leading you to do something, you can know He has a good reason for it. He sees and knows what you cannot see. If you will follow Him, the Holy Spirit will take you exactly where you need to go and help you reach your maximum potential in life.[2]

This concept became solidified in my spirit when I thought of the following explanation and analogy. My oldest daughter, Madyson, owns a horse, and I see the trust in the relationship the two of them have. Although her horse weighs more than a ton and could easily pull away and run off, because she trusts Madyson and has a relationship with Madyson, she follows Madyson's lead. This is the sort of trust that should characterize our relationship with the Lord and our yieldedness to His plan.

When I first started making this shift in my own life, I thought through how I wanted to live and how I needed to change my thinking in order to change the decision track I was on. I have used this method, writing out who I am and want to be, many times in my life to make changes in my life. I write out the way I want things to be, but in the present tense. Here is what I wrote out to begin changing my thinking in order to change my decisions.

A quick note: at the time I was trying to stop myself from making my own financial decisions and investments. You will recognize that from what I wrote. I titled it "This Is His Plan" and read this outline regularly for several months until I changed my life and became what I wrote.

- Be extremely disciplined about only doing what I know to be true.

- Do not buy or sell unless I know.

- He holds it all in His hand. He knows what's going up, what's going down. He knows when things will peak, when things will drop.

- Trust Him. Rest in Him. Follow Him.

- Follow His leading every time. Do not trade just to trade.

- Must be very disciplined to move only when He says move. Not before, not after, not early, not late; only when it's time.

- When it's time, do it with full trust, full confidence that it is right.

- Do not force anything. Do not second-guess. Do not doubt.

- He knows everything before it's going to happen. Follow Him.

- John 16:13 says, "He [the Holy Spirit] will shew you things to come." The Holy Spirit shows me things to come. He shows what's going to happen before it happens. He shows me what to buy and when to buy it. He shows me what to sell and when to sell it.

I literally reread what I had written out every day. I thought about it and meditated on it until it became part of who I was. This happened over a period of several months, but I finally got to the point where I stopped leading and allowed the Holy Spirit to lead the show. After a year or two of disciplining myself to do only what the Holy Spirit showed me to do, I realized that the Lord was not leading me to trade in the stock market. I am not saying that the stock market is bad. What I am saying is the Lord had already predetermined methods or vehicles that He specifically prepared for me to use at set times.

It has been several years since this realization, and the Lord has not spoken to me once about investing in the stock market. However, He recently spoke to me about buying a specific piece of land and prepared me to buy more real estate. So that and that alone will I do. This is what He has for me. You need to find out what He has for you.

The Holy Spirit can absolutely be trusted by you to be your personal GPS. The Holy Spirit can be trusted to be the one with the rope in His hand, leading you through the plan of God for your life. Trust Him, be in tune with Him, and you will live a life full of goodness and adventure, far surpassing anything you could have ever dreamed up for yourself.

Chapter Eleven

401(K) AND FREAKING OUT

S EVERAL YEARS AGO Michele and I had started reading a few books on how to improve the way we handled our finances. We were looking to make a few improvements with our finances, and we did pick up a couple of things that have worked for us. These books talked about widely accepted, sound financial planning advice. They talked about things like college tuition for the kids, 401(k)s, retirement, and so on. The more I read, the more I realized that I was not prepared financially for college tuition for my kids and that my 401(k) was not even close to where it needed to be according to sound financial advice (man's financial advice).

Please don't get me wrong. Some of these books offer some good, natural ideas and actions that you can take financially. Many of these things I already knew, having received my finance degree from a very good business college. I also knew that if you started setting aside a certain amount of money at the age of twenty years old, you would have a very large sum by the time you are in your early forties. Of course, I had not done that. We had put some away, but it did not meet the standards of sound financial planning. Please keep in mind this sound financial planning is man's way, and under that system alone there is neither knowledge of nor access to the benefits of tithing, which is *the blessing* of the Lord.

So here I was approaching forty, and as I looked at our finances they were nowhere near where they told me it should be. I thought about my oldest daughter attending college in a few years with two more kids right behind her and started to freak out on the inside. What had I done? I let go of many of the financial things that I had been taught, things that I should have been doing all along. The more I would read, the more I began to sweat, realizing that according to financial counsel I had totally missed it. The more I read these books the more I began to freak out on the inside about our financial future.

In the natural, it's not like I could reverse time. What had I done? Had I really been a good provider to my family? I was pretty quiet about it on the outside, but on the inside it was like a flood of worry and doubt that just poured all over me. I felt like I had failed as the provider for my family. What was I going to do? College would begin in a couple of years, and I wasn't ready.

From the age of nineteen, I knew that God had already met my needs, but I was still making my own financial decisions up until that point. Although it wasn't totally clear to me at the time, I was trying to meet my own needs. Let me put it this way: I was walking in faith, I was tithing, and I was putting a demand on the Word and receiving from the blessing. We lived well financially. However, I had not been doing what financial advisors would tell me I should have been doing. The next two paragraphs are short, but the truth of them changed my life forever. I reread this and meditated it until it got deep, deep, deep into my spirit and changed my thinking. I then accepted it as the only truth and fully cut myself off of the world' system in the area of meeting my own needs and fully cut over to the Kingdom of God's system—and have never looked back. If you are struggling in this area, you need to highlight the following section and reread it until it gets in you and then make a decision never to look back.

> Man's way is to try and meet his own needs. But God never created man to meet his own needs. God created man so that *He* could meet man's needs and be his God. The world will tell you that *you* need to provide for your own need and for them (the masses that don't serve God); they are right. But that's not us! God's plan has always been and will always be to meet *all* of our needs and for us to live in the *best* of the blessing. *He* wants and has *already* provided for *all* of our needs—all of them.

This one truth totally set me free. God did not create you or I to meet our own needs. The Lord wants to meet our needs. He wants to be our God and take care of you and I. Now there are some that will take this to the extreme and use it as an opportunity to live a lazy life. That's not at all what I am saying. For the individual believer pursuing the Lord's plan (and tithing is part of His plan; that's where He gets to pour His blessing on you), that individual will find themselves in the center of the will of God where the grace of God and goodness of God abounds.

James 2:20 says, "Faith without works is dead." Another way to say that is "faith without corresponding action is dead." You can believe God all day long, quote Scripture until you're blue in the face, and run around the church until you're out of breath. But if you don't put some corresponding action to your faith it will not work. If you are in faith, standing on His Word, and your actions are in line with what you believe, then your faith will work and you will receive the promise.

I will add one more thing here: ask the Holy Spirit what action you can take that would be in line with what you are believing. If you ask Him, He'll show you. When He does, do what He shows you. It's just that simple.

So here I was, I had been saved and walking in this faith thing since the age of nineteen. I had been tithing, studying the Word, and endeavoring to fulfill the plan of God. I was approaching forty, and for about two months I was completely freaking out on the inside. After some time I went back to the Lord, and He reminded me that these people that are writing these books on natural finances do not have a covenant with the Almighty God. They truly *are* on their own and *must* meet their own needs. But that wasn't my situation; that was just their situation.

I began to think about the Lord and the fact that He wants to meet all of my needs. As I began to meditate, I began to think about what the Lord owns, and what I have access to through my covenant with Him. For the next several months I would meditate on the Lord's extreme wealth, riches, and on the unlimited resources that belonged to Him. You see, a natural man without a covenant does not have access to any of the Lord's resources. But a man who has a covenant with the Lord has access to *all* of it! If you understand the concept of dominoes and the plan of God for your life, then you know that college tuition for my children did not sneak up on the Lord. He already had things planned out for my children. In His Kingdom, college tuition, room and board, books, and everything they will ever need have already been provided for in the Kingdom.

The Lord already has the college picked out and paid for. He also has your first job or business domino prepared and your spouse picked out too! Young people, listen. God already has your soul mate picked out for you, and at the right time, in one of your dominoes, you will walk into that domino and have a marriage that is off the charts amazing! These heaven-on-earth marriages are available to everyone, but only a small per-centage of people actually have them because they date the wrong person, get involved in a way they shouldn't, and so on. Outside of getting saved, this is the single most important decision you could ever make. The Lord has a tremendous plan and future for you!

There is a domino in all of our futures that has college tuition in it (along with every other event in our lives). For tithers that believe God, walk in love, and follow the leading of the Holy Spirit, you *will* walk right into your preplanned dominoes of good. Don't freak out. God has an abundance of resources available to you in His Kingdom.

Chapter Twelve

TWO REALMS BLENDED TOGETHER

I F YOU ARE a new Christian, I am going to cover some deep stuff in this chapter. "Two realms blended together" refers to the natural realm and the spiritual realm that we live in. Every thing I teach is founded on the Word of God. To that end, let's lay some foundational scriptures to get us started.

> The earth is the LORD's, and the fulness thereof.
>
> —PSALM 24:1

> And if children, then heirs; heirs of God, and joint-heirs with Christ.
>
> —ROMANS 8:17

> Giving thanks unto the Father, which hath made us meet [able] to be partakers of the inheritance of the saints in light.
>
> —COLOSSIANS 1:12

When you read these three Scriptures, they are telling you first that the Lord owns everything in the earth. It all belongs to Him. All the silver, all the gold, all of the real estate, all of the oil—all of it. The entire earth, including everything that is valuable, belongs to the Lord.

Romans then tells us that not only do we have a covenant with God, and not only are we His children and He our Dad, but we are heirs with God and joint heirs with Jesus. What does it mean to be a joint heir? It simply means this: everything that Jesus owns, we own too.

Colossians tells us that we were made able to participate and partake in this inheritance that the saints co-own with Jesus. Let me put it very simply. When you asked Jesus to be the Lord of your life, you came into a covenant relationship with Him. He owns and has access to everything you have and you are, and reciprocally you own and have access to everything He has and everything He is.

In regard to Colossians 1:12, I had been asking the Lord, "If I own this inheritance with the Lord, where is it?" There are just some things the Lord will not reveal to you unless you inquire of Him. Well, He answered me and said, "Your inheritance is in the light". Isn't that what Scripture says? Our inheritance is in the light, and the Lord put financial resources in the earth—all at the same time.

OK, I need to lay a little bit of science down on you. We know the Scripture says that God is light. Science tells us that light travels at 186,282 miles per second, which is way beyond what our natural eye can see. As a matter of fact, science tells us that we can only see about 3 percent of light, which means that *we cannot see* about 97 percent of light with our natural eye.[1] Think about that. We actually only see a very small percentage of light. Why? Because it is moving too fast.

We also know that God lives in eternity. When God first made man, man was created to live forever on the earth. When sin came into the earth, so did death and thus time. Hebrews 9:27 says, "It is appointed unto men once to die," yet we also know that once man dies, his spirit lives forever somewhere in eternity.

Here is how I explain it to my kids. For simplicity sake, we live in an "earth bubble." Time only exists inside this earth bubble. God, however, is eternal, and He lives outside of time. He always was, is, and will always be. Since He sits outside of time, He knows the end from the beginning. We live in a body that is subject to time, but our spirit man was created to live forever for eternity somewhere, either with the Lord or without Him (heaven or hell).

For years I sought the Scriptures asking the Lord to reveal these things to me, especially in the area of finances. I first began to get some real understanding while meditating Malachi 3:10. It says:

> Bring ye all the tithes into the storehouse, that there may be meat in mine house, and prove me now herewith, saith the LORD of hosts, if I will not open you the windows of heaven, and pour you out a blessing, that there shall not be room enough to receive it.

One day the phrase *windows of heaven* jumped off the page at me, and the Lord spoke to me and said the words, "Access to." The scripture says that when you bring your tithes He will *open* the *windows of heaven*. Let me give you an example. If you are sitting in your house or your apartment, then you are living in an area, or dimension. If you open your window and stick your head out or climb out the window, you have now entered another area or dimension that you were not previously in. The Lord spoke to me and said that when I tithe, it gives me access to the realm of the spirit, where there is no time or space and a full supply of riches in glory. The Kingdom of God is not just in heaven way up in the sky; it is all around me. It is also within me. There is no space or time in heaven. Body parts are in this realm, wealth is in this realm, revelation—not information—is in this realm. All that heaven has is in this realm, and when I tithe, it is opened up and made available to me. I have full, total, and complete access to it. By faith, I take what I want and need.

I then wrote these words in my Bible: "Heaven is open to me. Free, total, and complete access to all of heaven's resources are available to me here and now in the earth. The tithe opens this realm to me. Now I operate in this realm for all that is wanted or needed."

This is when I first began to see and understand that we live in two, dimensional realms blended together. The natural realm that we know all too well is filled with limitations, natural boundaries, and the slowness of time. And the spiritual realm is where all of heaven's resources are in abundance, where all things are possible, and where what we call miracles are everyday, normal occurrences; this is in the Kingdom of God. Tithing gives me access to this spiritual realm. It opens it up and makes it readily available to me.

Take a look at the following scriptures. I believe they will help you.

> God is light, and in him is no darkness at all.
>
> —1 JOHN 1:5

> If we walk in the light as he is in the light, we have fellowship.
>
> —1 JOHN 1:7

> For by him were all things created, that are in heaven, and that are in earth, visible and *invisible* [invisible to the natural eye].
>
> —COLOSSIANS 1:16, EMPHASIS ADDED

> Who hath called you out of darkness into his marvellous light.
>
> —1 PETER 2:9

For ye were sometimes darkness, but now are ye light in the Lord: walk as children of light.

—EPHESIANS 5:8

Giving thanks unto the Father, which hath made us meet to be partakers of the inheritance of the saints in light [the inheritance is in the light].

—COLOSSIANS 1:12

The eyes of your understanding being enlightened.

—EPHESIANS 1:18

And to make all men *see* what is the fellowship of the mystery, which from the beginning of the world hath been *hid in God*, who created all things by Jesus Christ.

—EPHESIANS 3:9, EMPHASIS ADDED

The kingdom of heaven is at hand.

—MATTHEW 10:7

In whom [Christ] are hid all the treasures of wisdom and knowledge.

—COLOSSIANS 2:3

Who only hath immortality [referring to Jesus], *dwelling in the light* which no man can approach unto; *whom no man hath seen, nor can see*: to whom be honor and power everlasting.

—1 TIMOTHY 6:16, EMPHASIS ADDED

When the Kingdom of God shows up in the natural realm, the light changes with it. In Acts 9 we read the story of Saul's encounter with the Lord. Verse 3 says, "And as he journeyed, he came near Damascus: and suddenly there shined round about him a *light* from *heaven*" (emphasis added). In Acts 12 we read the story of how Peter was imprisoned and an angel came and delivered him out of prison. Verse 7 says, "And, behold, the angel of the Lord came upon him, and a *light* shined in the prison" (emphasis added). We know that the angel walked him out of prison. At the end of verse 10 it says, "Forthwith the angel departed from him." Peter is in prison and all of a sudden the angel shows up out of nowhere to help

Peter. Once Peter is out of prison, the angel just disappears. But did the angel actually disappear, or was Peter no longer able to see him? Let me ask you this, Just because you don't see the angels with your natural sight, does it mean they are not present?

We know Psalm 34:7 says, "The angel of the Lord encampeth round about them that fear him, and delivereth them." Scripture says you have an angel with you at all times, next to you, in close proximity of you. We know from Scripture that you do. But have you ever wondered where he is? He's in the light. He's in the spiritual realm; he's in the part of the light that your natural eye cannot see. He's there, he's present with you, but you just can't see him with your limited, natural sight.

When we read about an angel appearing to people in the Scriptures, how is that happening? I believe one of the ways it happens is that we live in a slowed-down earth where we think going ninety miles per hour on the highway is fast. But when compared to the realm of the spirit, it is incredibly slow. I do not pretend to understand everything here, but there are some things the Lord has shown me in the Word. When angels are seen, I believe they are slowed down to match the speed of our lives here on earth and what our natural eyes can capture. To us it seems like they just appeared or disappeared, but I believe what is happening is they slow down so that they can be seen for a purpose and then go back to normal light speed where they can't be seen by the natural eye.

Let's take Acts 8:39–40 as an example.

> And when they were come up out of the water, the *Spirit of the Lord caught away Philip,* that the eunuch *saw him no more*: and he went on his way rejoicing. But Philip was found at Azotus: and passing through he preached in all the cities, till he came to Caesarea. (emphasis added)

This is the story where Philip came alongside the eunuch. We know the story. Peter explained the Scriptures to him, the eunuch said he believed on Jesus, and they then stopped the chariot and baptized him in the water. When the eunuch came up out of the water, Philip was gone. Philip then appears up in Azotus. In the Christian circles we call it being translated.

What happened to Philip? The Scriptures tell us what happened: the Holy Spirit caught him away and brought him someplace else. I believe the Holy Spirit picked him up and took him for a ride and then dropped him off. The Holy Spirit is light, so when the Holy Spirit took Philip into the spiritual realm, how fast was Philip moving? At the speed of light. To the eunuch's natural eye, Philip just disappeared. But what I believe actually happened was that he moved so fast that the eunuch couldn't see it and then arrived so fast in Azotus that no one saw him coming. Once he got to his destination the Holy Spirit "dropped him off," and he went back to the speed of our lives here on earth, which is slow and can be seen by the natural eye.

How about the story of Elisha in 2 Kings 6? We know this story as well. The king of Syria was warring against Israel, but Elisha would hear what was being said in the king's chambers miles away. How can a man hear something miles away without technology? Naturally speaking, he can't! However, when you operate by the Holy Spirit, you are not operating by the natural realm but by the spiritual realm. Natural laws and natural limitations don't apply. Spiritual laws, which include spiritual hearing and spiritual seeing, override natural laws.

Elisha hears and tells the Syrian king's plan to the king of Israel. The Syrian king becomes infuriated and sends an army with horses and chariots to surround the entire city where Elisha is. When Elisha's servant sees the massive army, he begins to panic. He knows the army is present to capture Elisha, his master. Let's look at what Elisha said to his servant in verses 16 and 17:

> And he answered, Fear not: for they that be with us are more than they that be with them. And Elisha prayed, and said, LORD, I pray thee, open his eyes, that he may see. And the LORD opened the eyes of the young man; and he saw: and, behold, the mountain was full of horses and chariots of fire round about Elisha.

Let me ask you a question. When did the Lord's angels show up? Did they arrive moments before Elisha's servant saw them? No. They were there all along. Where were they? In light, in the realm of the spirit. The servant did not know that they were there until the Lord allowed him to see into the realm of the spirit. Once he saw them his whole perspective changed! I think sometimes the Lord slows things down for you to see them; other times I think the Lord allows your eyes to "speed up" so that you can see them.

Here's the point. *All of heaven's resources* that are promised in the Word are here, right here, in the realm of the spirit. Jesus said the Kingdom of God is *at hand.* Jesus came to reestablish the Kingdom of God in the earth to the same status of Adam before he sinned. But it also means that all of the Kingdom of God's resources are here and present with you now. They just happened to be in the realm of the spirit, which your natural eye cannot see, but they are oh so very real!

I laid out this entire foundation to specifically talk about where our inheritance actually resides. Where is our inheritance? It is in the light.

> Giving thanks unto the Father, which hath made us meet [able]
> to be partakers of the *inheritance* of the saints in *light.*
> —COLOSSIANS 1:12, EMPHASIS ADDED

Our inheritance is in the light. All of the resources that we could ever want and need are in the realm of the spirit, just like the Lord's army that was encamped around Elisha. All of the finances you will ever need are already paid for, sitting there and available for you. As a matter of fact, you own it.

> The earth is the LORD's, and the fulness thereof.
> —PSALM 24:1

> And if children, then heirs; heirs of God and *joint-heirs with Christ.*
> —ROMANS 8:17, EMPHASIS ADDED

> He that spared not his own Son, but delivered him up for us all,
> how shall he not with him also *freely give us all things?*
> —ROMANS 8:32, EMPHASIS ADDED

> For we walk by faith, not by sight.
> —2 CORINTHIANS 5:7

All of the resources in the earth (seen and unseen) belong to the Lord. You co-own all of it.

God has vast amounts of riches, healing, body parts, divine protection, and so on, waiting for you to access it. It is sitting here in the realm of the spirit, just waiting for you to access it. Just because you don't see your angel does not mean that he does not exist. And just because you don't see your inheritance in the light, does not mean it's not here. Your inheritance is here, just waiting for you to access it and use it.

In 2006 Michele and I decided to go to a Believers' Convention in Milwaukee held by Rev. Kenneth Copeland. I had been meditating on the scriptures above and had been listening to Brother Copeland and Brother Winston talking about the blessing and working the system (God's system). While sitting in the Great Lakes Believers' Convention, the Lord dropped this image into my thinking. This is the very first picture I ever drew, it reflects our inheritance in the light (Col. 1:12).

This is a picture or a representation of your co-ownership in the realm of the spirit. Here's what I wrote when I saw this:

> I co-own everything with God. I am a co-owner. It's all there in the realm of the spirit. I need to claim and call in what I want and need. Mark 11:23–24 says believe you receive when you pray. Believing is easy to do when you know it's been there from before the foundation of the world. It's *all* already there, it's all *already* been provided and given to me.

When I asked the Lord about this, I was inquiring about finances. However, you could easily draw into this picture health, body parts, divine protection, and any other promise you find in His Word.

To further illustrate my point, I am going to use a scene from a popular movie. My goal in this next section is to provide you with another visual, another way to relate or connect with what I am sharing with you. Some of you may think this is a little hokey, but when the Lord first began to reveal this to me, the scene in this movie is what helped me grasp the concept. In the movie *The Matrix,* the main character, Neo, goes on his journey of discovering who he really is. Throughout the movie he's being attacked by his enemy. As he opens his mind he progressively discovers who he really is and what his enemy really is. As he continually grows in this revelation of who he is, he gets stronger and stronger and begins to see the fabrication and deception of the enemy for what it truly is.

My point in telling you this story is to highlight my favorite scene in the movie, where Neo finds himself in the hallway with three agents (the bad guys). Neo begins to see into the other realm and sees his enemy for what they are. He begins to realize that he has *total dominion* over this other realm. He begins to see this other realm for what it really is, fear, or "false evidence appearing real."

As he begins to see the truth, he begins to control it and have access and dominion over it. The agents begin shooting bullets at him. Neo, with the revelation of who he is, takes authority over this lower realm and causes the bullets to stop in mid air and plucks them out of mid air. The agents attack him, and with almost no effort and seemingly superhuman speed, Neo single-handedly stops all three agents. These same agents beat the tar out of Neo in previous encounters. Now they know they can no longer defeat him.

Why do I tell you this story? Because in a sense, *you are Neo.* As you go to God and seek Him, inquire of Him, and ask Him to reveal His Kingdom to you, you will move over to operating in the realm of the spirit, and things will be significantly easier for you to believe. It will become easy to work your faith and pull these resources from the realm of the spirit into the natural realm and fulfill the plan of God.

When the Lord revealed this to me, it became so easy to believe Him for way, way bigger things that I ever could before. Why? Because I knew where it all was, and I knew it was there in abundance. I knew it belonged to me, and I knew how to access it—by faith.

Remember, the Lord said the Kingdom of God is at hand. All of the Kingdom's wealth and resources are available to you now.

Chapter Thirteen

KINGDOM OF GOD

I N THE PAST several years there has been a tremendous outpouring on the topic of the Kingdom of God. I am sure there are many ministers that have taught on this subject. However, there seems to be a couple of ministers that are on the tip of the spear as it relates to this topic. Dr. Bill Winston and Dr. Randy Caldwell are two men that have impacted my life in this area, men that I look to as leaders on this topic.

Although there is much to be said about the Kingdom of God, for purposes of this book I am going to summarize the message for you in this chapter. It is *the* key message for every believer and is key to understanding the rest of this book. It begins with this question and answer: Did Jesus come to save us from hell? Yes, of course, but there is so much more to it than that. In order to better understand, we need to go back to the beginning.

God created the earth and put mankind in charge, beginning with Adam. Genesis 1 starting in verse 26 and continuing to verse 28 lays it out for us.

> Let us make man in our image, after our likeness: and let them have dominion…over all the earth.…and subdue it [the earth]: and have dominion…over every living thing that moveth upon the earth.

God put Adam in charge of the earth and gave Adam all authority and dominion over the entire earth and everything in it. God's original plan was to extend the Kingdom of heaven to the earth and have His people rule and reign in the earth. God made Adam (mankind) the god of this world. Notice *god* is spelled with a little g. The Lord Jehovah is God with a big G, and He put Adam in charge of the Garden of Eden and in charge of the entire earth. Adam was in charge and had total dominion over all of the earth. This authority and power was given to him by the Lord God Jehovah Himself.

When Adam fell, he lost his position of authority and dominion in the earth. All power and authority that Adam had was handed over to Satan. In 2 Corinthians 4:4 it says:

> In whom the god of this world hath blinded the minds of them which believe not.

How did Satan become the god of this world? The Lord certainly did not make him the god of this world, but the Lord did make Adam the god of this world. When Adam sinned, Adam handed that title, authority, and dominion over to Satan.

So why did Jesus come to the earth? Yes, to pay the price of sin so that sinners could be saved from eternal damnation. However, the *primary* reason Jesus came to the earth was to preach and establish the gospel of the Kingdom of God.

What is the message of the Kingdom of God? Here it is: Jesus came to the earth to reestablish our authority and dominion in the earth. The position that Adam once held and lost (as the god of this earth), Jesus took back from Satan, and He has put us back in that position of authority and dominion in the earth! In so doing, Jesus has reestablished the Kingdom of God in the earth. We who love God and are called by His name, we are in charge and have total dominion in the earth.

> All power [authority] is given unto me in heaven and in earth. Go ye therefore.
> —Matthew 28:18–19

> Which he wrought [worked] in Christ, when he raised him from the dead, and set him at his own right hand in the heavenly places, far [far, far, far] above all principality, and power, and might, and dominion, and every name that is named, not only in this world, but also in that which is to come: And hath put all things under his feet, and gave him to be the head over all things to the church.
> —Ephesians 1:20–22

> And hath raised us [you] up together, and made us sit together in heavenly places in Christ Jesus.
> —Ephesians 2:6

Jesus already had all authority in heaven, but He did not have all authority in the earth. He gave it to Adam, and Adam gave it to Satan. Jesus came, paid the price, and took "all authority" back for the purposes of the earth. And He gave it back to us! We are seated in Christ at the right hand of the Father. We are back in charge of the earth! He expects us to run the show down here in the earth. We are now citizens, sons (and daughters), and ambassadors in the earth. We are:

- Citizens of the Kingdom of heaven, here in the earth,

- Sons and daughters of God, having an intimate relationship with our Dad, and

- Ambassadors representing God's government here in the earth.

Jesus came to save that which was lost. People who are lost need saving, and only Jesus saves. However, that's not the only thing that was lost. Adam and Eve lost their position of authority and dominion in the earth. Jesus paid the price for sin *and* He paid the price and bought back our authority and dominion in the earth. Jesus made a way for every sinner to get saved *and* has now reestablished us who are washed by His blood to take our rightful place in the earth. The gospel of the Kingdom of God is that we who believe on Jesus are to rule and reign in the earth under the Lordship of Jesus Christ.

Chapter Fourteen

MOVE OVER MICROSOFT. KOGOS IS HERE.

T
HE MESSAGE OF the Kingdom of God is that Jesus put us as believers back in charge of the earth. Satan doesn't like this fact and will do everything he can to distort, discredit, and dismay you from believing this reality. God is waking us up to this truth, and it will forever change your life.

If you are saved, then you know that there is a Kingdom of light and a kingdom of darkness. These two kingdoms both use systems or ways of operating in their respective kingdoms. As you can imagine, these two systems and governments are radically different. Prior to you being saved, you were under the domain and influence of the kingdom of darkness. The enemy has a system that he uses to run the world and to run people. In order for you to be part of reigning in the earth under the leadership of the Lord Jesus, you are going to have to learn the differences between these two systems. More importantly, you are going to have to learn how to work God's system and be disciplined to learn to stop using the world's system.

In order to explain these two systems, I am going to use a technology analogy. If you read the Scriptures, then you know that Jesus used analogies all the time. He talked about farming, sowing and reaping, and so on. In those days, the masses understood these concepts. Well, we live in the information age, the high-tech age—so we are going to use some high-tech analogies to help you understand how the Kingdom of God operating system (KOGOS) works.

If you have ever owned a computer or a laptop, then you probably know that the computer came with an operating system. This operating system is a set of rules that dictates how the computer is to work and how information is to be moved, shared, extracted, and governed. The laptop will not work correctly if there is something wrong with the operating system. As a matter of fact, there are things that you can do to crash the operating system and thus the computer. If you can understand that a *laptop* is governed by an *operating system*, then you can also understand that the *earth* is governed by an *operating system*.

I want you to think about the following example for just a moment. You have a laptop, and you can chose one of two operating systems (OS). Below I have depicted the two most well known OS's.

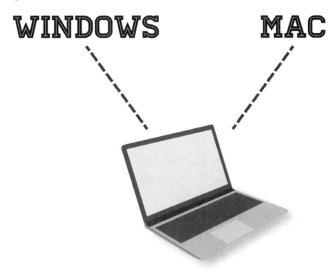

In this example, you can choose either the Windows operating system or the Mac operating system. The operating system that you chose is what's going to govern how that laptop will work and how it will perform the functions you ask of it. The OS's are different and thus do not operate the same way. There are things you can do with a Mac that you just can't do with a PC that runs Windows. I'm not picking on either OS; I am simply trying to illustrate a point for clarity.

If you can understand this concept, then you can understand that God created the earth and put one operating system in the earth, which I have called KOGOS. When Adam fell, he gave authority and dominion over to Satan, and Satan devised his own operating system to govern the earth, which I have called WOS, or world's operating system.

Kingdom of God Operating System = KOGOS

World's Operating System = WOS

A non-believer only knows and has access to WOS. It isn't until a person becomes a believer that they realize that there is another operating system that exists, called KOGOS. KOGOS operates radically different than WOS, yet a person must use one OS or the other at any one given time to access the earth's resources.

WOS is available to everyone, believers and non-believers. KOGOS, however, is only available and recognized by believers. Therein lies the challenge for believers. WOS is a known operating system, and KOGOS is not. Each of these operating systems has different sets of rules that govern how the earth's resources are accessed and managed.

However, KOGOS totally dominates WOS in every respect of the word. A believer that uses WOS is still subject to Satan's domain and rules, and as a believer, he doesn't like you. Why? Because he's trying to establish his kingdom, and you don't belong to him. He knows that a believer who uses KOGOS totally dominates WOS and thus Satan. Satan has absolutely no recourse and is rendered powerless against KOGOS.

First Corinthians 1:25 says, "Because the foolishness of God is wiser than men [WOS]; and the weakness of God is stronger than men [WOS]." What does that mean for you and I? It means the entry-level KOGOS user can dominate and outperform the master WOS user. To make this very plain, the least skillful KOGOS user will outperform the most skillful, super intellectual WOS user. Yup, that's what I said. And like with anything, if you give yourself time at it, you can progress from an entry-level user to a moderate user to an advanced user and then finally to a master user.

Unfortunately, most believers are still using WOS and don't even realize it. The purpose of this book is to teach every believer how to effectively use KOGOS so that you can establish heaven's reality in your life. From there, we as a collective force can continue by expanding the Kingdom of God in every area that God leads us in.

At a high level, I want to expose some of the differences between WOS and KOGOS. This is by no means a comprehensive list but rather a sampling for you to compare and consider:

WOS	KOGOS
Man's ways	God's ways
Operates in the natural realm	Operates in the spiritual realm
Basic system, lots of problems	Perfect system, works every time
Subject to external forces	Total dominion over all situations
Subject to time	Ability to override time
Subject to natural laws	Ability to override natural laws
Information	Revelation
Work with sweat/toil	Sweat-less success
Work/invest time for money	Sowing and reaping
Learning	Wisdom downloads
Limits	Limitless
Social and economic boundaries	No boundaries/you rule
Medical science	Divine healing/divine health
Producing externally	Producing internally
Personal and man-made protection	Divine protection (angels)
Limited to natural sight	Seeing and knowing in the spirit
Limited resources/your ability	Unlimited resources/KOGOS provided

I want you to picture the earth with all of the resources that you could ever need inside of it. In the earth, there are a vast amount of resources, such as gold, silver, natural resources, buildings, transportation, businesses, oil, lands, jobs, finances, etc.—an abundance of all things valuable. However, in order to get to these resources, you knowingly or unknowingly must choose an operating system first (man's way or God's way, WOS or KOGOS). Once you pick an OS, then information or resources can be moved and managed according to the rules of the OS you chose. Non-believers can only chose WOS. Believers have their choice which OS they want to use; they can chose either WOS or KOGOS.

WINDOWS   MAC

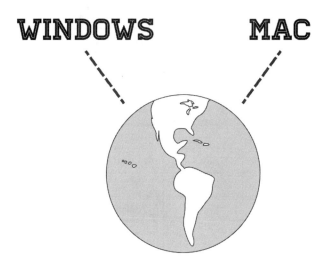

We have described WOS to some extent already. As you probably already know, WOS does not work very well. It is riddled with bugs, glitches, and is highly unstable, causing crashes for the user. This OS is bound to natural laws such as time, distance, race, age, social, economic, and individual biases. In this system things are built up, and when the storms come they are easily knocked down and swept away. This system is very cyclical, which means there are highs and lows; there are good times and bad times, which makes WOS very unstable and unpredictable to operate. WOS is governed by Satan and was founded and built upon an infrastructure called sin.

KOGOS, on the other hand, is only available to believers. KOGOS is also commonly referred to as the God's way operating system. This system is absolutely perfect. There are no bugs, no flaws, no glitches. It is absolutely flawless and works every time. This system was created by the Creator of all things. It is governed by spiritual laws or sets of rules that are timeless, spaceless, and it sits on top of and overrides all natural laws. In this system, the natural laws that govern WOS do not apply to KOGOS. They are two totally separate and distinct operating systems that have no commonality other than they are both OS's and are used by people to access the earth's resources.

In KOGOS, there are no limits as to how far you can expand and accelerate this operating system. As a matter of fact, the Christians that are using KOGOS and living in the good life are just scratching the surface and yet still getting amazing results. There is no limit as to how far and how hard you can push KOGOS; it is limitless and endless. It can do things and commands that Christians have never even dreamed of yet. Why is that? Because the one that invented and created this operating system is none other than the Lord, the Creator of all things. The Lord is perfect and has no flaws or defects. That is why His operating system is perfect and limitless. KOGOS is perfect because it is built upon an infrastructure called righteousness.

KOGOS is built upon the Rock, so when the storms come—also known as computer worms and malicious attacks—they are smashed against the Rock and never even make it to the operating system. Let me put this to you another way: when a believer uses KOGOS in their life the enemy is rendered helpless, and you become unstoppable. It's like you live in this bubble, a bubble of blessing, a bubble of protection. When using KOGOS you are invincible and untouchable.

There are three governing laws that dictate how KOGOS works:

- Walk in love
- Believe God
- Be led by the Spirit of God

Other attributes that govern this operating system are policies such as "all things are possible to him that believes" and "with God, nothing is impossible." (See Matthew 9:23 and Luke 1:37.) When comparing this to WOS, things are based on greed and selfishness, and there are many impossible situations and requests that cannot be answered or fulfilled.

When you accepted the Lord Jesus as your Savior, you had KOGOS downloaded into your spirit. You immediately became a co-owner and equal partner in the Lord's company. And the best part was, Jesus paid for the investment!

When you bought into Jesus, the Lord not only brought you in as a user, but He brought you in as an investor and co-owner in His company. The Lord is the CEO, and you are the co-COO, the chief operating officer. He expects you to master His operating system and to operate it and push it as far as you can to establish His Kingdom in the earth.

For millions of Christians, even though they have full access to this operating system, and even though they co-own the company, they are *still using the old operating system* from the competitor. Does that make any sense to you? For most, they don't even realize that they're doing it. They are just so used to the old operating system that they just stay with what they know. You see, the majority of Christians in the earth today are using WOS to access and manage the earth's resources.

Let me state that again. Most Christians and all non-believers use WOS. Only a small percentage of Christians are actually using KOGOS. That's the reason so many Christians read about how amazing the Kingdom of God is and the incredible and supernatural results it will yield, but they very seldom get the results themselves because they're using the old operating system. WOS will never produce what KOGOS can produce. If you want to get God's results, then you need to use His system. It just doesn't work any other way.

Below is a picture I drew when the Lord first began explaining how KOGOS and WOS work as it relates to the earth. At the top of both systems you will see the labels for God's system and man's system. God's system (KOGOS) is based on the blessing of the Lord. You will see that only Christians (represented by halos) can use KOGOS and access and manage the earth's resources. At the bottom, you will see man's system (WOS), which both non-believers and believers have access to. They use WOS to try and access the earth's resources. This system is under the curse, and Christians that use this system get the worst of it. Satan, who runs this system, is not interested in helping you one bit.

Take some time to really evaluate this picture and think through how this works. Put yourself in each system and ask yourself, What happens when I use WOS? What happens when I use KOGOS? Ask the Holy Spirit to reveal this to you!

GOD'S SYSTEM

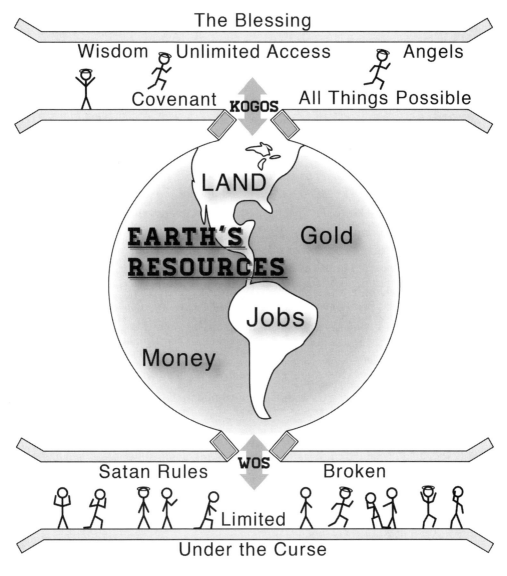

MAN'S SYSTEM

Now that we have established the two operating systems, I want to talk about some of my mistakes. I have always found it easier to use firsthand experiences to help bring things to life and make them real. And since I have made many mistakes, I have plenty of good stories to tell! Let's see if you can relate to some of my shortcomings.

As a Christian, I found myself moving in and out of the two different operating systems. For many of the areas in my life I was using KOGOS. I was tithing. I was walking in love. I was using my faith for several areas, such as healing, and even believing God for biblical prosperity. However, when I saw opportunities to make financial gains I would get out of the KOGOS and shift over to WOS. How would I do that? I would make my own decisions, which would send my life in a direction based on those decisions. I was not self-aware and did not realize I was doing this. I would be believing God, but anytime I would hear financial conventional wisdom, I would just take off and do it and not even inquire with the Lord as to what KOGOS would have me do. Every time I did this, I would shift out of KOGOS and into WOS.

As I look back, I mostly did this when it came to money. I would shift out of taking it to the Lord and following the leading of the Holy Spirit and into using my mind only and making decisions based solely on my natural thinking and what conventional wisdom said. I don't know why, but for some reason when it came to making money I would believe God for the promise of the blessing but then go try and make it happen on my own. I would rely solely upon my natural mind, which of course is WOS, and WOS is subject to all of the flaws, limitations, and crashes of that system. There is no supernatural insight by the Holy Spirit into financial matters when you operate using WOS.

After doing this for many, many years, Michele and I had finally had enough. We knew there was far more than what we were accessing and living in, and it had to be something on our end that needed to change. We got to a point where we said to each other, *"That's it. No more! If the Holy Spirit doesn't lead us to do it, we're not doing it!"* We had reached our limit of frustration and were done with trying to make things happen on our own. We drew the line in the sand, and that's when I took my hands off the wheel of my life forever. If the Holy Spirit didn't lead me to it, I didn't want it.

There's nothing wrong with listening to good, well-meaning people. However, the goal here is to get to a point where you can be led by the Holy

Spirit and follow His leadings and promptings for your life. In other words, grow up from being a spiritual baby to being able to stand on your own two feet as a mature, responsible spiritual adult. (See Ephesians 4:11–16.)

For the first time in our lives, Michele and I fully cut over to one operating system for every area in our lives. We absolutely refused to use WOS ever again, and it was really simple for me to figure it out too. How did I do that? I asked myself one key question: Am I leading the charge, or are the Holy Spirit and His Word leading the charge? That will tell you real quick what OS you're using.

From that day forward we have fully operated in KOGOS. I'm happy to report that although we are still human and can miss it, we have made no big mistakes and have been exceedingly blessed because of it! This is also where our journey began. This is where everything in this book started. It was because of the decision we made to follow the leading of the Lord in every area of our lives that we have seen these things unfold in front of our eyes and are able to articulate these concepts that we have lived out for many years now.

After reading this, if you realize that you are partially or fully using the wrong operating system in your life, the good news is you can begin learning how to use KOGOS today. The Lord will help you to fully move over to KOGOS for every area of your life. You might as well! You co-own the company with the Lord, and you are the chief operating officer of this operating system. It's a matter of trust. Trust Him.

Chapter Fifteen

TAKE YOUR SPOIL

NOW THAT WE have established the difference between KOGOS and WOS, let's dig deeper into how you need to access all of the Kingdom of God's resources and bring it into the natural realm. Tithing puts your name on it and makes it all available to you. However, it's your faith that brings it from the spiritual realm into the natural realm. As you begin and continue to meditate in the Word of God in this area, God will begin to increase your sight so that you can see the promise of God. And *if you can see it, you can have it.*

In this chapter I'm going to teach you how to *take the Spoil in order to build the Kingdom.* I'm going to draw on two areas that the Lord has spoken to me to make this very clear. The first is from a dream the Lord gave me, and the second is an excerpt from a book I read. I am going to provide you the detail of both areas and then summarize how to take the spoil at the end of this chapter.

On May 4, 2010, I had a dream from the Lord, and I woke up seeing and knowing the following:

> The *Word of God* spoken is the *key* that *opens* up the *Kingdom* to a man (or woman) in the earth.

I want to clarify this, though: It is not the *logos* Word that is the key. It is the *rhema* Word that is the key. So let me restate what the Lord showed me and add the rest of it here:

> The *rhema Word* of God spoken is the *key* that *opens* up the *Kingdom* to a man (or woman) in the earth.
>
> WOS is contained and has boundaries in the five natural senses, but KOGOS does not. The Word of God spoken is the Key that opens up the Kingdom of God and all of its limitless resources and power to a man. The Word of God is not part of the world's system; it sits outside of it and above it. Man's words and ways are naturally in line with the world's system

94

and are subject to all of its limitations and shortcomings. WOS is a broken, evil, doomed-to-fail system. God's Word spoken supersedes all of that, being from the ultimate kingdom, the Kingdom of God.

How does the Word of God go from a *logos* Word to a *rhema* Word? When you take the time to meditate His promise, His Word. As you ask the Lord to reveal it to you and you seek Him, there will come a time when that promise is revealed to you and you will *see it*. When you see the promise, that's when it becomes *rhema* Word. How else does someone become "fully persuaded"? When you take the time to meditate on His promise, you'll see it and know it and become fully persuaded that promise is yours. No one will be able to talk you out of it.

How does a promise become a *rhema* Word that you can see? I like what Brother Bill Winston says on this topic.[1] These are my summary notes:

> Meditating the Word will cause you to *see* what you can't see. Meditating will cause three things to happen to you:
>
> 1. Your boundaries will be affected.
> 2. You will make different decisions based on what you see.
> 3. Your personal recognition system will start working.
>
> Meditation destroys the old image and the old boundaries so you can see the Kingdom of God. And when you can see it, you can have it.

You have been trained since your childhood to think according to natural laws. But when you became born again you entered into a new family and a new spiritual realm that was not available to you. Non-believers only have the natural realm, but not you! However, if you don't take the time to think these things through by mediating in the Word, then your thinking will be based on your natural thinking, which has many, many natural limitations. Why is this a big deal? Because your *thinking* is tied to your *believing*.

> As he [a man] thinketh in his heart, so is he.
> —PROVERBS 23:7

When you meditate on a promise to a point that you see it in your spirit, *then it's yours*. Once you know that you know it's yours, you simply declare and call in what already belongs to you. That's what the Lord was telling me when He told me that the Word of God spoken is the key that opens the Kingdom's resources and brings it from the realm of the spirit into the natural realm.

Faith is what makes the Kingdom of God operate. You first need to see the promise of God through the eye of faith. Once you see it, you call it in until you have it. The *logos* Word is like having a chain with a bunch of keys on it. At least you have the keys. That's a good start. However, when you're standing in front of a specific door that you want opened, having all the keys to the neighborhood won't help you at that moment. You need the specific key that opens a specific door. That's what the *rhema* Word does for you! When you get the Word in your heart to a point where you can see it, then it will be the key that will open that door of promise for you.

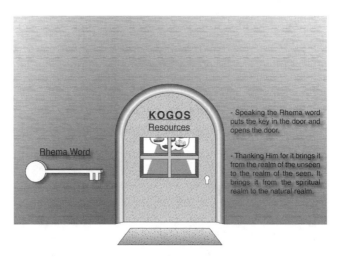

The *rhema Word* of God spoken is the *key* that *opens* up the *Kingdom* to a man (or woman) in the earth.

This is the first part, but let's tie this into how the rest of KOGOS works as it relates to taking your spoil.

This next section comes from the mini-book called *How God Taught Me About Prosperity* by Kenneth E Hagin. At the time, Rev. Hagin had been pastoring a church and living in the parsonage. Brother Hagin was led by the Lord to leave pastoring and go into field ministry to hold revival meetings and was really struggling financially. He went to the Lord in prayer to inquire about his financial struggles and quoted Isaiah 1:19 to the Lord: "If ye be willing and obedient, ye shall eat the good of the land." The excerpt from this section begins with the Lord speaking in a still, small voice to Rev. Hagin's spirit saying:

> "The reason you are not eating the good of the land is that you don't qualify. You are *obedient*, but you are not *willing*. So you don't qualify to eat the good of the land."
>
> The Lord said to me, "Go back to the Book of Beginnings"... "You know I made my man Adam?" He continued.
>
> "Yes."
>
> "Adam originally was the god of this world. He ruled and dominated it. That's the way I planned it. When Adam sold out to Satan, then Satan became the god of this world (2 Cor. 4:4). I'm not withholding adequate food and clothing from your little children—that's not Me! It's the devil. He's the god of this world. [The god of WOS.]
>
> "The money you need is on the earth. I'm not going to rain money down from Heaven. I don't have any money up here. And if I did rain money down, it would be counterfeit, and I'm not a counterfeiter. The silver and gold are down on the earth where you need it."
>
> "Then what should I do?" I asked.
>
> "In the first place," He replied, "don't pray anymore about money the way you have been praying.
>
> "**Number one**, claim whatever you want or need, because it's down there on the earth. And Satan has the most control of it."
>
> "Now, Lord," I said, "I can believe that You want to meet our *needs*—but our *wants*?"
>
> "He replied, "You claim to be a stickler for the Word. In the 23rd Psalm it says, *'The Lord is my shepherd; I shall not WANT'* (v. 1). And it says in the 34th Psalm, *'The young lions do lack, and suffer hunger: but they that seek the Lord shall not WANT any good thing'* (v. 10).
>
> "**Number two**," the Lord continued, "say, 'Satan, take your hands off my money.' It's Satan who is keeping it from coming to you—not me. And **number three**, say, 'Go, ministering

spirits, and cause the money to come.' Ministering spirits are sent to *serve* you. Did you ever read in the Book of Hebrews where it says that angels are '*ministering spirits, sent forth to minister FOR them who shall be heirs of salvation*' (Heb. 1:14)?"

I could see it then: for years, angels had been standing around me doing nothing because I had never told them to do anything.[2]

Brother Hagin went on in the book to talk about how he would cry and weep during his prayer time and barely pay the bills. He realized what he had been doing and corrected it immediately by claiming the amount of money he needed, binding the devil, and sending his angels to bring the money to him. He not only received the money he needed that week, but it worked time and time again.

As I read this entire section by Rev. Hagin, I began to write out the gems that I saw below:

- Brother Hagin was led by the Lord to go into the field; he did not go on his own.

- He was obedient but had to adjust his willingness, his attitude.

- The Lord told him he was praying wrong. Could you be praying wrong?

- He was praying wrong because of wrong thinking. Could you have wrong thinking in an area? If so, it will impact your faith.

- God put Adam in charge. That was and will always be His plan.

- Adam gave authority over to Satan.

- Satan set up a system (WOS) and is in control of most of the earth's resources.

- Jesus took authority back and gave it back to us. He gave us a system to implement called KOGOS.

- KOGOS totally overrides WOS, the devil, and his demons.

- God is not withholding anything; it's the devil.

- God put an abundance of financial resources in the earth for you to use. There is no shortage of resources.

- The devil acts like a schoolyard bully that owns the place, but the reality is, he does not own anything. You do!

- What do you need to do to a schoolyard bully? Punch him in the nose. Then he'll back off. *You* own the place, not him.

- If you live your life according to KOGOS, you get to claim what you want and need. KOGOS works every time. Learn how to work it.

I'm big on outlining steps to success. Jesus came to reestablish God's word to Adam in Genesis: "Let them have dominion." He gave us a totally superior system called KOGOS for us to use to establish His Kingdom in the earth.

Satan is nothing more than a schoolyard bully. He doesn't own the earth or any of its resources. He runs WOS, but Jesus gave you KOGOS, which totally dominates WOS. When dealing with Satan, the only thing you need to do is bind him with your words. That's it. Tell him to take his hands off your money. This is what I mean when I say to punch him in the nose. Scripturally, we find this in Matthew 12:29 and Mark 3:27. I have added some wording in parenthesis:

> No man can enter into a strong man's house [schoolyard bully], and spoil his goods [it's actually your stuff; he's just in control of it], except he will first bind the strong man [KOGOS dictates that you bind him with your words; you don't need to do anymore than this]; and then he will spoil his house [you render him powerless from preventing the financial resources from coming to you and you get the resources you claim].
>
> —MARK 3:27

So there are three steps KOGOS says you need to do to take your spoil.

1. Claim what you want or need. It's all there already. Pray, "Lord, I am believing you for _____. I claim _____ and believe I receive it now in Jesus' name." I would first meditate the promise of God that you are believing for

until it becomes a *rhema* Word to you. Once you see the promise, then claim it. The *rhema* Word will open that door to you.

2. Bind the devil. Say, "Satan, take your hands off of _____." Once you open the door, the schoolyard bully is obstructing your possession of it. When you bind him, you render him powerless.

3. Dispatch your angels. Say, "Go, ministering spirits and cause _____ to come to me." In KOGOS, angels are assigned and work for you. Put them to work.

Yes, it is just that simple. Don't overcomplicate this. Start putting KOGOS to work for you. It's time to take your spoil so you can have the resources to establish the Kingdom of God in the earth.

I'm big on providing visual depictions. In the picture below David was using KOGOS, and he overcame the best that WOS had at that time, Goliath. Naturally speaking, it looked like WOS was way stronger, way bigger, and way more powerful than a person using KOGOS. However, KOGOS dominates WOS every time.

KOGOS

This is what it looks like with our natural eyes when a person using KOGOS encounters WOS. Naturally speaking, it doesn't look good. It doesn't make sense, and everyone is scratching his or her head, saying, "There's no way this could ever work out in my favor." But if used correctly, it does every time.

Remember, there are two realms, natural and spiritual. Goliath is a natural giant, and he represents the enemy and any obstacle or situation that seems way too big for you to overcome. Satan would have you believe that he's running the show down here and that he owns the earth.

However, that is simply another lie. The earth and all of its resources belong to the Lord. The Lord put Adam in charge. Adam was not deceived but gave all authority over to Satan, which put him in charge. Jesus came to the earth, died, and rose for us and took all dominion back and gave it to you and I. He restored us back to what His original plan was. We are in charge. You are joint heirs with Christ, which means the earth and all of its resources belong to you.

I'm going to give you a parable, or an analogy, to help you understand how Satan fits into this equation. Satan is the schoolyard bully. Have you ever dealt with a schoolyard bully? They are not fun, but you cannot ignore them because they are not going away until you deal with them. Imagine playing basketball on the schoolyard playground, and as you are playing your ball rolls away from you. You run over to pick it up, but the schoolyard bully picked it up and doesn't want to give it back. The ball belongs to you, but he's trying to bully you and prevent you from getting your ball back.

This is a picture of Satan in the earth. What is the ball? The earth is the ball, and Satan doesn't want to give it back to you. If you think about this situation naturally speaking, you might be inclined to think that you are much weaker than him and have no chance against him. *The key to this whole equation has to do with what operating system you are using to retrieve the ball.* If you use WOS, you have no chance. He runs WOS, and you are definitely not on his team. He'll make sure the other WOS users that are working for him get money and resources to establish his kingdom, and you will get very little.

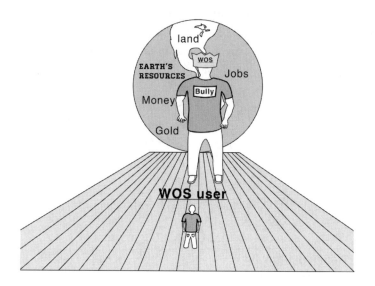

However, when you are using KOGOS, you are an absolute giant next to him. He may act tough, but he's actually afraid of you. Have you ever been around a bully that acts all tough, and then someone bigger and tougher comes around? The bully still tries to act kind of tough, but deep down he's actually afraid. That's what happens when you shift from WOS to KOGOS. You go from a total wimp to being a total GIANT. He has no chance of stopping you.

The only thing he can try to get you to do is to believe his lies. He'll tell you things like: money is bad and the root of all evil, that he owns the earth and is in charge down here, that you're just an old sinner, that poverty is a badge of honor and humility, and so on. If he can get you to believe that, then you won't believe the truth and you won't act on the truth—and *he stays in control of the ball.*

As a KOGOS user, you are enormous next to Satan. *You are the giant,* not him. When you bind him with your words, it's like zapping him with a *taser.* You paralyze him and render him helpless against you, short term. He may be holding the ball (the earth's resources), but when you bind him, you paralyze him, and he drops the ball. You then simply send your angels in to retrieve it. That's how KOGOS works. *The schoolyard bully is powerless to someone using KOGOS.*

Remember the book *Heaven Is for Real*? Earlier I described how God allowed the boy to see an image of how Jesus shoots down power on you. That's what Deuteronomy 8:18 is talking about; it's describing when a believer uses KOGOS. As a KOGOS user, you are the giant, and you have all of heaven's resources backing you! With His anointing already on you to get wealth, you just need to issue your commands and take your spoil. That's how it works.

Let me give you one more example that I think will really help drive this home in your thinking. I want you to imagine that you own a very large company. When you are the owner of the company things are very different than being an employee. You decide what direction the company goes in and when you want things done. You don't hope the employees will do it; you provide them with clear instructions on what is needed and when it is needed by. I'm not talking about being mean. I'm talking about speaking from a position of authority and clarity on what you want accomplished and when it is to be completed. The employee's job is to see to it that these tasks are completed by the deadline.

In this example, the company is the earth, and you own it. The employees are the ministering spirits sent forth to minister to those that are the heirs of salvation. That's you. As long as you are in line with the Word of God and speaking the Word of God, think of your angels as your employees. They are there to help you get the job done, but they won't do anything unless you give them tasks from the Word of God to accomplish in your life.

Romans 8:19 says, "For the earnest expectation of the creature [the earth] waiteth for the manifestation of the sons of God." Scripture is saying that the earth is waiting for the sons of God to take their rightful place in the earth as the ones in charge. Verse 21 says, "Because the creature [the earth] itself also shall be delivered from the bondage of corruption into the glorious liberty of the children of God." Scripture is saying that the earth shall be delivered from their hands (WOS) and into our hands (KOGOS). If you're still not sure it's yours, just look at 1 John 3:2, which declares, "Now are we the sons of God."

You see, KOGOS deals with things in the spirit. The natural just follows. The natural realm is a slave to the spiritual realm. However, you still need to do your part naturally. You deal with it in the spirit, and then you do the necessary natural things to walk it through the process. Your actions need to correspond with what you are doing spiritually. If you have a sales job, you still need to make the phone calls, do the proposals, and meet with clients. If you deal with it in the spirit first, these other things become much easier, and you get KOGOS results.

I like what John 15:7–8 (NKJV) says, because it pulls it all together: "If you abide in me, and My words abide in you, you will ask what you desire, and it shall be done unto you. By this My Father is glorified, that you bear much fruit; so shall you be My disciples."

OK, let me summarize how KOGOS works to take your spoil:

1. Claim what belongs to you and believe you receive it.

2. Bind the schoolyard bully.

3. Send your angels in to retrieve it.

What areas in your life are you believing God for? Have you done steps one, two, and three? If not, put them in motion now. You'll be glad you did! This is just like someone using a computer and issuing the command Control–Alt–Delete. This command will result in the computer being rebooted. The same idea holds true in KOGOS! The KOGOS user needs to issue their KOGOS commands to *take your spoil*.

Chapter Sixteen

FAITH CONTAINERS

NOW THAT WE have laid the foundation of the earth and the two operating systems (KOGOS and WOS) that govern the earth, let's talk about how much of the spoil you get to take. Let's look at what the Scriptures have to say about you having access.

> Bring ye all the tithes…if I will not *open* you the *windows of heaven*, and pour you out a blessing.
> —MALACHI 3:10, EMPHASIS ADDED

> Let us therefore *come boldly* unto the throne of grace, that we may obtain mercy, and find grace to help in time of need.
> —HEBREWS 4:16, EMPHASIS ADDED

> By whom also *we have access by faith* into this grace wherein we stand, and rejoice in hope of the glory of God.
> —ROMANS 5:2, EMPHASIS ADDED

> In whom we have boldness and *access with confidence by the faith* of him.
> —EPHESIANS 3:12, EMPHASIS ADDED

> For through him [Jesus] we both have *access* by one Spirit unto the Father.
> —EPHESIANS 2:18, EMPHASIS ADDED

> To the praise of the glory of his grace, wherein he hath made us *accepted* in the beloved.
> —EPHESIANS 1:6, EMPHASIS ADDED

> For there is no respect of persons with God.
> —ROMANS 2:11

We are His children, and we have been accepted in Him. This means that by faith we have access to Him. Romans 8:17 says we are joint heirs with Christ, which means we co-own everything with Him. Our tithing gives us access to the inheritance, but our faith brings it in. Let's elaborate on that.

Matthew 9:29 tells us, "According to your faith be it unto you." This tells me that I will receive according to what *I* believe. Proverbs 23:7 tells me, "For as he thinketh in his heart, so is he." This tells me that my believing and faith are directly tied to *my thinking*. In Malachi 3 it says that God will pour out His blessing upon us, so much so that we will not have room enough to receive it. The Word tells me that *the results* of the blessing need room or a place or a container to receive it. And when you put all these Scriptures together, they tell me that I determine the size of the container to receive and walk in the blessing of God.

God will pour out His blessing upon you, but *you* will determine the size of your container to receive it. We will call them faith containers. *The size of your faith container determines how much you keep.* How do you increase the size of your faith container to keep more? When you meditate on the Word of God, you expand your faith container, which allows you to keep more of the promise of God in your life. Below you will see examples of the different-sized containers that a believer can have to receive the blessing of God.

Spoon

Teacup

Tall Glass

Barrel

Dump Truck

Warehouse

The Word of God tells us that the blessing of God will fill us to over-flowing. What many Christians fail to understand is that *they* determine the size of their faith container, which determines how quickly it fills up to overflowing and how much of it they keep and walk in.

In addition to that, there are different-sized containers for the different promises of God. You can have a large bowl or even a bucket-sized faith container in the area of your healing and walk in a level of divine health but only have a Dixie-cup-sized faith container as it relates to finances or another area in the Word of God. If you are not walking in and are not keeping much of the promise of God in an area, don't get mad at the Word, God, or at your pastor. It's just time to trade up your faith container. Get in the Word, find His promises in that area, and meditate it until you can see the promise in a greater capacity in your life. Once you are able to see in a greater capacity, you have now traded your smaller faith container for a larger faith container. The greater your capacity to see it, the larger your faith container is and the greater amount of the blessing you get to keep and walk in.

People try to make it harder than it is, but the truth is simply that if you don't like the size of your faith container, don't get mad or think you have to stay there. It's time for you to trade up for a bigger one!

The children of Abraham did not enter into the Promised Land because of their unbelief. They disregarded one of the keys to God's operating system, and that is to believe Him. Why was their belief not intact? Because they saw themselves as grasshoppers. They did not see themselves as children of the Most High God who had a covenant with Him. The only way to rectify this is to spend time in His Word and meditate on who you are in Christ. The only thing that stopped them was how they saw themselves.

When you got saved, you became a new creature in Christ. You now had the ability to switch off of the old and broken-down operating system (WOS) and start using this new, perfect, and fast operating system (KOGOS). However, for most people, the image on their computer screen did not get refreshed. So they still see themselves and think in terms of who they used to be. It's time to refresh the image on the computer screen, the image of how you see yourself and who you are on the inside. You refresh by meditating on His Word and allowing the Holy Spirit to create for you His image of who you are in Him.

Remember, when accessing all of the vast resources in the earth, there are three governing laws that we must be in line with. They are: 1) walk in love, 2) believe God, and 3) be led by the Spirit of God. A believer that stops making his own decisions and making his own plans and moves over into seeking the Kingdom of God and His right-standing will begin to have all these things added to him. Tithing allows you to participate, but the *rhema* Word of God is the key that opens the door and brings these resources from the realm of the spirit into the natural realm and into your hands. If you are lacking in an area of your life, meditate on the promises of God in your heart until you see it in your spirit. Once you see it, it's easy to believe that it belongs to you, to declare His promise, and to call it in to you.

As you begin to grow and mature in understanding and learn how to operate effectively in this system, you'll go one step further. Before you do anything you will inquire of the Lord and ask Him where the answer is in His Word to receive the promise.

Let me give you an example: in a very short amount of time I was presented with two opportunities to buy some land. We were generally interested in buying but had learned over the past several years not to make our own decisions in these areas. So I asked the Lord what was going on and what He wanted me to do. I felt prompted in my heart to read Deuteronomy 8, and as I read verse 1 the words *possessed the land* jumped off the page at me. Not only did it jump off the page, but it went off in my spirit. I knew that not only was I supposed to buy both pieces, but one of the purchases was more complicated and involved, and He gave me the exact how-to, to buy the land.

In other words, I asked the Lord first, and He told me specifically how much to offer and how to structure the terms of the deal. So that's what we did. I took that *rhema* Word, and I declared and called it in. I received the Word and said things like, "In the name of Jesus, I possess the land. Thank you, Lord, that the land is mine. I receive it now. I thank you for it."

If the how-to is not prompted in your spirit, then your response is simple: Leave it alone. It's not for you to do. You need to understand that God is constantly doing two things for you. He is *providing* for you, and He is *protecting* you. When you follow Him in the yes's, He is providing for you. When you follow Him in the no's He is protecting you. It's just that simple. He is walking you into the path of blessing and keeping you away from the traps of the enemy.

The *rhema* Word of God spoken is the key to the Kingdom and all of its resources. When you are in the plan of God, also known as being divinely positioned, you are in a place where God has totally set you up for His goodness.

How much goodness can you have? As much as you want! The resources in the Kingdom of God are unlimited. There is no limit to the amount of riches, wealth, and resources in the Kingdom. In addition to the unlimited amount of finances available to you, there is an unlimited amount of everything you could ever need in the Kingdom. You need healing? It's in there. You need a specific body part replaced? It's in there. You need a new car? It's in there. If the Word of God promises it, then the Kingdom of God contains it in total abundance and overflow.

So who determines how much you can have? You do. More specifically, your faith does. If you can see it in your heart, you can have it. If you can't see it, you can't have it. This is not because it is not available to you but because believing in your heart and saying it with your mouth is how you access it. Most people go directly to just saying it, and they don't want to do the extra work it takes to put the promise in their heart. You have to allow the Holy Spirit to paint the image of it in you so you can see it, and that takes time on your part to do. Once you see it, you know it's yours. The saying part becomes pretty easy.

Let me give you an analogy. The game of baseball has three principles to it—throwing, hitting, and fielding. The batters that are on deck are in the batter's box, and they are practicing their swing. They are studying and perfecting their swing so that when they get into the batter's box they increase their probability of hitting the ball. When it's the batter's turn he steps into the batter's box. Now the game is on. The batter is no longer practicing his swing; he is up at the plate in the batter's box, and he is there to hit the ball and get on base. It is no longer a matter of just swinging the bat. The batter needs to wait until he can *see the ball*. Once he sees the ball in a manner that looks really good to him, *that's when he swings the bat*. He has no opportunity to hit the ball and get on base until he first sees the ball.

In this analogy, swinging the bat is like declaring the Word of God. Seeing the ball is when a believer has taken the time to meditate the promise of God until they see it in their heart. In order to get on base in the Kingdom of God and score points, you must do both. You must see the *rhema* Word of God and then declare what you see. When a player does these two things together, he or she will get on base and score points.

Mark 9:23 says that all things are possible to him who believes. So I ask you, what do you believe? Most people don't realize it, but their thinking is the problem! Many that were not raised in "this faith thing" still think about who they were, what they had, and what they could do according to the definitions and rules that governed the old operating system. In that old operating system, they were defined as no good, not pretty enough, not smart enough, can't do that, will never happen for you, too old, too young, wrong upbringing, and so on. For many, these definitions did just that—they defined us. It told us how we could live, where we could live, who we could marry, how much we could make, and what we could do. It boxed us in and limited us to a small domain. However, when we got saved, these definitions no longer applied to us. We became and are now new creatures in Christ, the old is passed away and behold, everything is new (2 Cor. 5:17)!

So wherein lies the challenge? The challenge is to identify when you are thinking in the old system (WOS) and continually replace the old operating system's definitions with the new operating system's definitions (KOGOS). For good or for bad, this is a process that happens over time. Your spirit is reborn immediately, but your mind, a.k.a. your thinking, is not. It needs to be reprogrammed, or better yet, redefined. This new operating system has new rules and new definitions for you. You will be amazed when you continue to learn who you already are, what you already have, and what you can already do. The more you can see in the Word, the larger your faith container becomes and the more of God's promise you walk in.

Chapter Seventeen

HOW IT WORKS

THE COMPANY I worked for invented great technology that was both innovative and complicated. When we first began to meet with potential customers we had a difficult time explaining how the technology worked, and thus the potential customer was uncomfortable. It's only human nature that if people don't understand how something works they are less likely to believe in it and thus less likely to buy it. Shortly thereafter, the company created a document that we shared with potential customers titled "How It Works." Customers began to understand much faster, with understanding comes confidence, and with confidence customers began buying.

This same principle is also true in our Christian faith walk. God does not require us to live by blind faith, but rather if we'll meditate on the Word of God, the Lord will reveal it so you can see it and thus strengthen your faith.

In Proverbs 24:5 it says, "A wise man is strong; yea, a man of knowledge increaseth strength." Allow me to translate into simpler wording: *understanding how something works makes your faith stronger.* In this chapter I am going to lay out the fundamentals of "how it works" as it relates to the tithe and the prayer of faith.

A short time a go one of the hockey dads on my son's hockey team gave his heart to the Lord. We had a great discussion one night not quite a year after he got saved, and he shared with me that he was tithing. I was so impressed, because for many men trusting the Lord with their finances is a difficult thing.

My friend was an executive with a big company, and the tithe represented a fair amount of money. As we spoke he knew that he needed to tithe, but I could tell he did not totally understand why, how it works, and the benefits to him. The next morning while sitting in church I was prompted by the Holy Spirit to text him the following, which I call "The Tithe 1, 2, 3."

The Tithe 1, 2, 3: How It Works

1. You bring the tithe (Mal. 3:10–11).

2. Jesus receives the tithe (Heb. 7:8; 4:14).

3. Jesus puts spiritual power on you (Deut. 8:18).

As you bring the tithe up to Him, He puts His power on you. This spiritual power is scripturally called *the blessing*. Why does He do this? The blessing (spiritual power) is to cause you to rise above your natural limitations in order to financially prosper you. He wants to be your Provider and for you to *use His power* to bring in finances that, naturally speaking, you cannot do on your own. Out of your abundance you finance the Kingdom of God.

It's just that simple. Yes, you should tithe because the Bible says so. But when you bring Jesus something (the tithe), He brings you something (His power). Now that you understand it, believe it and operate in it.

You bring the tithe to the Lord,
the Lord puts His power on you.

Tithe

When you bring the tithe to Him, He puts spiritual power on you. Good things begin to be drawn to you. Proverbs 10:22 says, "The blessing of the Lord, it maketh rich, and he addeth no sorrow." However, you don't have to stop there. That is just an entry-level benefit. You can now use this spiritual power on you in conjunction with the prayer of faith. In this book, "Take Your Spoil" is the prayer of faith.

Remember, there are some fundamentals that you need to be in line with as you become more skillful in operating God's system. Always be aware of and in tune with 1) walking in love, 2) believing God, and 3) being led by His Spirit.

THE PRAYER OF FAITH: HOW IT WORKS

To help explain and describe this section, I'm going to refer to a book called *A Place Called Heaven*, written by Dr. Gary L. Wood. This book is an incredible account of how Dr. Wood died as a young man, visited heaven, and then returned to earth and lives with us today.

I first heard of this book when a guest minister referred to it in a recent visit at our church. I have learned over the years to judge everything against the Word of God. Below is the excerpt from the book that God used to explain to me how the prayer of faith works. I will follow it up with a broader explanation and then the Word of God to confirm it.

This story begins while Dr. Wood is being given a tour of heaven:

> After we left the nursery, we walked into a long building, much like a storage building. I was caught off guard by what I saw hanging from the walls. There were rows of legs, rows of arms, cubicles with hair and eyeballs of various colors. Every part of one's anatomy was in this room. You might be wondering, why does there need to be a place like this in heaven? It reminds me of the joke, "Were you out of the room when God was passing out brains?" John [Dr. Woods friend that had previously died was his heavenly tour guide] knew that I didn't understand, and he told me to watch what happens. Before my eyes, from my heavenly vantage point, I could see the prayers of the saints below shooting up like arrows towards heaven. Angels would receive the prayers and bring them into the throne room of God. God would grant the prayer request, and the angel would be dispatched from that room to deliver the miracle. If a doctor says that something is no good and must be removed, I'm telling you that God has a miracle for you. God has a spare parts room! You say, "Well, I know people who needed a miracle. They may have even asked for one, and did not receive it."

Let me tell you what I saw next. I saw the angels dispatched with the answered miracle from God, fighting principalities and powers, only to be stopped by doubt and unbelief from the mouth of the petitioner. Such things as, "It's not for me," or "It's not God's will that I be healed" is what I heard them say. Then the angel would sadly turn around and take the miracle back to heaven and deposit it into a room called unclaimed blessings. I have read the New Testament over and over and have not once found where Jesus turned anyone away saying, "No, it is not my will that you be healed."[1]

When I read this account, the Lord began to speak to me and connect the dots for me. He brought up scriptures to me in the Word to further elaborate on what this account describes, as well as pictures to make it very plain so that I could understand how it works.

First, I want you to know that there are storage buildings, storehouses, or huge warehouses in heaven full of everything good that you could ever want or need. If Jesus paid the price for it, and it is promised in the Word, then know that it is being stored for you in these warehouses in heaven.

He that spared not his own son, but delivered him up for us all, how shall he not with him also freely give us all things?
—ROMANS 8:32

Bring ye all the tithes into the storehouse.
—MALACHI 3:10

If there are natural storehouses in Kingdom of God in the earth, it stands to reason that there are storehouses in the Kingdom of God in heaven. Where are these storehouses?

The eyes of your understanding being enlightened; that ye may know what is the hope of his calling, and what the riches of the glory of his inheritance in the saints, And what is the exceeding greatness of his power toward us-ward who believe.
—EPHESIANS 1:18–19

> But my God shall supply all your need according to his riches
> in glory by Christ Jesus.
>
> —PHILIPPIANS 4:19

Dr. Wood saw what looked like a storage building where there was a full supply of all health-related things. I believe there are multiple storehouses in heaven for the different categories of the promises of God. A storehouse full of health, a storehouse full of finances, a storehouse full of wisdom, a storehouse full of peace and strength, etc. The benefits of every promise of God are stored in a storehouse, just sitting there waiting for believers to access them.

Dr. Wood does not offer the sign of the name of this place, but the Word of God has given the name of this place. It is called "riches in glory."

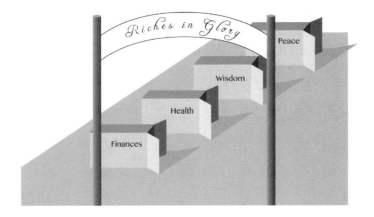

There is a place in heaven called "riches in glory" with storage buildings full of the promises of God for the saints of God. This is part of your inheritance *now*. How do you access it? With the prayer of faith.

Dr. Wood's account lays out how it works, as does the Word of God:

1. A believer prays in faith.

2. An angel brings it before the throne of God.

3. God, our loving Father, always says yes to what He has already promised to us in His Word.

4. God dispatches His angel to go to "riches in glory."

5. The angel picks up the fulfillment of the promise and begins the transportation of it to you.

6. The opposing kingdom attempts to stop the angel from delivering the promise of the Word of God to you.

7. You bind the enemy and remove the obstruction.

Here is a picture of how the prayer of faith works:

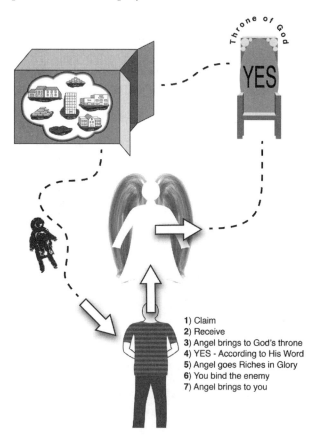

1) Claim
2) Receive
3) Angel brings to God's throne
4) YES - According to His Word
5) Angel goes Riches in Glory
6) You bind the enemy
7) Angel brings to you

Did you notice that it was not the enemy that prevented the fulfillment of the promise of God? As you learn how to become skillful in operating KOGOS, you will dominate the enemy and his kingdom. The devil can try to interfere and slow things down, but he cannot stop the operation of faith.

What stops the operation of faith? Doubt and unbelief coming out of the petitioner's mouth. Once again, you are in control, not the enemy. When doubt and unbelief come out of your mouth, you stop the angel and send him back to heaven. The angel then brings the fulfillment of your promise to a place called unclaimed blessings.

What is the prayer of faith? Referring back to "Take Your Spoil," it is the following:

1. Claim what you want or need. It's all there already. Pray, "Lord, I am believing you for _____. I claim _____ and believe I receive it now in Jesus' name." I would first meditate the promise of God that you are believing for until it becomes a *rhema* Word to you. Once you see the promise, then claim it. The *rhema* Word will open that door to you.

2. Bind the devil. Say, "Satan, take your hands off of _____." Once you open the door, the schoolyard bully is obstructing your possession of it. When you bind him, you render him powerless.

3. Dispatch your angels. Say, "Go, ministering spirits and cause _____ to come to me." In KOGOS, angels are assigned and work for you. Put them to work.

What should you do as a believer after you have prayed the prayer of faith but before the natural manifestation of the promise? You thank Him that it's already yours. Some might wonder if this is lying. If you understand what's happening, then you know that things are moving from the unseen realm into the seen realm.

The Kingdom of God operates in both the spiritual realm and the natural realm. Now you understand how your faith takes it from the unseen realm into the natural, seen realm. By meditating the Word of God and understanding how it works, your faith will become and remain strong. Strong believing and understanding will keep doubt and unbelief from being in your heart and will keep it out of your mouth.

Where is your inheritance? It is located in "riches in glory." Following the illustration is a list of scriptures from this chapter that will help solidify your understanding of how the prayer of faith works. Meditate on them and allow the Lord to use them to give you a *rhema* Word.

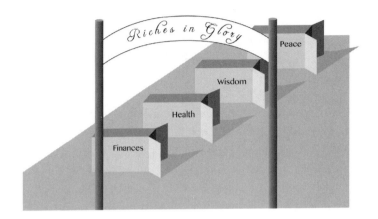

- Romans 8:32
- 1 John 5:14–15
- Mark 11:23–24
- Hebrews 4:16
- Malachi 3:10–11
- Ephesians 1:18–19
- Philippians 4:19
- Colossians 1:12
- James 5:15

Chapter Eighteen

THE KOGOS BUBBLE

I F YOU ARE experiencing difficulty in your life, it comes from one of two areas. Many Christians don't understand what these two areas are, let alone how to overcome them. If you read about the promises of God but live in very little of it, this chapter is for you.

The two areas that have the potential of preventing you from living in the fullness of the promises of God are:

1. The curse

2. Attacks

Rev. Nancy Dufresne wrote a wonderful book called *Causes: Since we're redeemed from the curse of the law, how come Christians fail?* This section begins by Rev. Dufresne explaining how an unbeliever is in rebellion to God's Word and as such, has no protection from the curse. An unbeliever is totally exposed to the curse and because they are under the curse, they have sickness, financial challenges, and a host of other problems.

Rev. Dufresne continues with Galatians 3:13, which states, "Christ hath redeemed us from the curse of the law…" As believers, we have been redeemed and are free from the Lordship of the curse. She than poses a very important question, a question that in times past I have often quietly wondered to myself:

Since we as Christians have been redeemed from the curse, why do Christians experience sickness, financial crisis, failures, and other problems?

> It's not because of the same reason unbelievers face these problems. Unbelievers have these problems because they are under the curse. But believers are free from the curse so why would believers face some of these same difficulties? Ephesians 4:27 tells us why. *"Neither give place to the devil."* Believers face difficulties unnecessarily because they give place to the devil.

Notice that the Ephesians 4:27 says, *"Neither GIVE place to the devil."* He can't take a place in you; you have to give him a place. You can open the door to the devil. The devil can't do anything to you anytime he wants to. If he could, then why would he have to deceive you first? Satan is the deceiver. He has to deceive you into believing the wrong thing before he can work the wrong thing in your life. He can't take a place in your life unless you give him a place by opening the door to him.

If you give place to the devil, and open the door to him to gain access to your life, then you can take that place back from the devil by closing the door to him and ridding him of access to your life.

It's to be understood, however, that just because you may be facing a test or a trial, doesn't mean that you're failing, and it doesn't mean you've opened the door to the devil. Even when you're in the will of God, the enemy is going to attack you. Difficulties are going to come your way because the devil seeks to hinder your progress in God's plan for your life.

It's one thing to be *attacked because you're progressing in God's plan,* but it's another thing entirely to *open yourself up to an attack of the enemy because of disobedience to God's Word.*

Even if you do miss God and open yourself up to an attack, if you will judge yourself and repent, making the needed changes, you can receive victory and come out of that difficulty.

To be "tested" and to "fail" are two different things. The enemy will attack and test you, but victory belongs to you every time, so the test shouldn't result in failure. But if there is failure, there's a cause.[1]

The scripture is very clear that if we as Christians fail, there is a cause.

For this *cause* many are weak and sickly among you, and many sleep [die early].
                                    —1 CORINTHIANS 11:30, EMPHASIS ADDED

Rev. Dufresne summarizes by stating that if we as Christians are weak or sick, or die early, we have given place to the devil somewhere. Deal with it right away! When you begin to notice things are not right, repent, close the door to the enemy, and continue on in victory. If we open the door, we must close the door!

When things are not going right in our lives, it's one of two things. We have either opened the door to the curse, or we are being attacked to try and stop us from fulfilling the plan of God. I'm going to share some personal stories about our life that I hope will help you in your life. Before we discuss the curse, we are going to highlight the promise of God, *the blessing!*

For years, Michele I knew we were living in a bubble. *What kind of bubble?* you may ask. The kind of bubble that is described and defined in the Word of God and is available to everyone! If this is the first time you are hearing this, it may be because you've never seen it in the Word or you never experienced it firsthand. Psalm 91:1 provides a good description of the bubble:

> He that dwelleth in the secret place of the most High, shall abide under the *shadow of the Almighty.*

This verse says that for a believer that lives his or her life with their heart close and connected to the Lord, they will live with a shadow, a covering, a hand, a bubble, or a force field from the Lord that encapsulates their life. I call it the KOGOS bubble, because if you are living this way, you reap the benefits of having the shadow or the bubble of the Lord around your life.

God says in His Word that if you keep your heart close to Him and follow Him you can live in the *blessing* and *protection* of God in and around every aspect of your life. You do not have to live in the curse as others do. The curse is attached to the world's system (WOS). We live in the earth, but what system we choose to live by is up to us! If you follow God's plan, or as I like to call it, the Kingdom of God operating system (KOGOS), then you can live in the blessing and protection that KOGOS provides.

There are bad things out there, but if you live in the KOGOS bubble, bad things can't get to you. It sees you—and you see it—but it has no access to you. The KOGOS bubble consists of two primary powers or forces. They are the blessing and the protection of God. The blessing of God is *offensive power.* The protection of God is *defensive power.* You need both to win in life. There are two sections of the Scriptures that I believe provide the most detail on this topic:

KOGOS Blessing	KOGOS Protection
Deuteronomy 28:1–14	Psalm 91
Offensive Power	*Defensive Power*
And it shall come to pass, if thou shalt hearken diligently unto the voice of the Lord thy God, to observe and to do all his commandments which I command thee this day, that the Lord thy God will set thee on high above all nations of the earth: And all these blessings shall come on thee, and overtake thee, if thou shalt hearken unto the voice of the Lord thy God. Blessed shalt thou be in the city, and blessed shalt thou be in the field. Blessed shall be the fruit of thy body, and the fruit of thy ground, and the fruit of thy cattle, the increase of thy kine, and the flocks of thy sheep. Blessed shall be thy basket and thy store. Blessed shalt thou be when thou comest in, and blessed shalt thou be when thou goest out. The Lord shall cause thine enemies that rise up against thee to be smitten before thy face: they shall come out against thee one way, and flee before thee seven ways. The Lord shall command the blessing upon thee in thy storehouses, and in all that thou settest thine hand unto; and he shall bless thee in the land which the Lord thy God giveth thee. The Lord shall establish thee an holy people unto himself, as he hath sworn unto thee, if thou shalt keep the commandments of the Lord thy God, and walk in his ways. And all people of the earth shall see that thou art called by the name of the Lord; and they shall be	He that dwelleth in the secret place of the most High shall abide under the shadow of the Almighty. I will say of the Lord, He is my refuge and my fortress: my God; in him will I trust. Surely he shall deliver thee from the snare of the fowler, and from the noisome pestilence. He shall cover thee with his feathers, and under his wings shalt thou trust: his truth shall be thy shield and buckler. Thou shalt not be afraid for the terror by night; nor for the arrow that flieth by day; Nor for the pestilence that walketh in darkness; nor for the destruction that wasteth at noonday. A thousand shall fall at thy side, and ten thousand at thy right hand; but it shall not come nigh thee. Only with thine eyes shalt thou behold and see the reward of the wicked. Because thou hast made the Lord, which is my refuge, even the most High, thy habitation; There shall no evil befall thee, neither shall any plague come nigh thy dwelling. For he shall give his angels charge over thee, to keep thee in all thy ways. They shall bear thee up in their hands, lest thou dash thy foot against a stone. Thou shalt tread upon the lion and adder: the young lion and the dragon shalt thou trample under feet. Because he hath set his love upon me, therefore will I deliver him: I will set him on high, because he hath known my name. He shall call upon me, and I will answer

afraid of thee. And the Lord shall make thee plenteous in goods, in the fruit of thy body, and in the fruit of thy cattle, and in the fruit of thy ground, in the land which the Lord sware unto thy fathers to give thee. The Lord shall open unto thee his good treasure, the heaven to give the rain unto thy land in his season, and to bless all the work of thine hand: and thou shalt lend unto many nations, and thou shalt not borrow. And the Lord shall make thee the head, and not the tail; and thou shalt be above only, and thou shalt not be beneath; if that thou hearken unto the commandments of the Lord thy God, which I command thee this day, to observe and to do them: And thou shalt not go aside from any of the words which I command thee this day, to the right hand, or to the left, to go after other gods to serve them. him: I will be with him in trouble; I will deliver him, and honour him. With long life will I satisfy him, and shew him my salvation.

Over the years Michele and I have talked about this many times. We didn't know exactly what it was, but periodically we would make comments like, "It seems like we are living in a bubble." When we started living in line with KOGOS, things just seemed to go easy for us. Other people would be struggling, but we would be prospering. Others would be facing difficulties, but for us things would just seem to go our way.

From our perspective, there were hard times, difficulty, and shortages around us; but in our life it was abundance, good things, and favor, with things just going our way. I'm not saying it is perfect and there are never any issues, but because we live according to KOGOS, the Holy Spirit directs us away from bad things and directs us into "good works" that the Father had planned from before the foundation of the world (Eph. 2:10).

Think of yourself and your entire life—everything that pertains to you, everything within your life's domain—in a self-contained force field bubble. Inside this force field bubble are all of the benefits of KOGOS. The blessing of God, which is God's power to prosper you, is on the inside of the bubble, while the outer shell or outer wall of the bubble is the protection of God, which shields you from the curse. The blessing of God applies to every area of your life, not just finances. The blessing of God impacts your finances, your health, your home, your children, your job, your business, your peace, your mental state of mind, and so on. The protection of God is an impenetrable wall of separation between the KOGOS user's life on the inside and the curse that is on the outside.

The movie *The Incredibles* is one of my favorites! If you've seen the movie, each family member has special powers. Violet's special power is that she can create a force field around her. In the beginning of the movie she kind of ignores it, but as time goes on she learns how to use it much more effectively. At one point she and her brother Dash are being chased by bad guys through the jungle. Violet puts her force field up, and the bad guys can't get to them because they are inside the force field.

Although it's not exactly this way, this is a type of example of what I'm explaining. This bubble of favor and protection is not temporary, however, and you can't just "throw it up" like Violet does. The KOGOS bubble works according to KOGOS. There are things you can do to make sure you keep the bubble sealed, and there are things you can do that will open the bubble and expose you to the curse.

The KOGOS bubble is real. All you have to do is read the Scriptures to see that it's real, and you *can* live in it, if you to choose to live according to KOGOS.

Michele and I have been living inside this bubble for many years now. From the outside looking in, people would say that we are some of the luckiest people they have ever met. I've always had favor on my various jobs. We believed God and live in a beautiful home. We have a great marriage and good relationships with our children. If there is a contest or prize to be won, my children put their faith out there and always seem to win them.

My kids have won bikes, laptops, and toys, amongst many other things. Recently we were at our church's youth camp, where they give away prizes, and my kids won stuff again. They specifically believed God for certain items and won them. We were in awe of how God works and incredibly thankful to Him. That night, the Holy Spirit said to Michele, "The reason you receive [win] stuff is because you *believe Me* for it. Nobody else does." Wow. Could it just be that simple? Yes.

At the age of ten, my oldest daughter, Madyson, began to believe God for a horse. At the age of thirteen, somebody gave her a horse. A couple of years later she wanted another horse that was trained a particular way, and we bought that horse a year later. My youngest daughter, Sydney, and son, Jordan, both loved to compete in sports, Sydney in basketball and Jordan in hockey. They both wanted to play elite level sports, so they believed God, worked hard, and both made the nationally ranked teams they wanted to play for.

Things just seem to work really well for us. There are minimal to no injuries or accidents, and our appliances and things around the house just seem to last a long time. Why is that? Is it because we are so good or perfect? Absolutely not. Trust me, I have plenty of things to work on. However, we have chosen to live a certain way—not our way but God's way. What is God's way? It's KOGOS. It's keeping your heart close and connected to Him. It's doing your best to live according to His Word. It's praying about decisions you need to make, asking the Holy Spirit to lead you into the plan of God for your life, and actually doing what He says and not what you think. When you develop a lifestyle of living this way, you will find yourself living in the KOGOS bubble.

Although we've been living in this bubble for many years now, I have definitely missed it a few times, and as a result I better understand how the KOGOS bubble works. The first time we missed it had to do with our tithe. Over a period of a couple of months we were estimating what my commission checks were and writing tithe checks based on these estimates. We fully planned to go back and make sure we had the exact amounts, but the busyness of life caused us to forget. Some time went by, and we began to recognize that things weren't going all that well. Things at home started breaking, and the sales for my job started to dry up and become much more difficult. This went on for several months and caused a lot of stress for Michele and I as we tried to figure out what was going on.

Michele later told me that every time she opened the checkbook she would hear on the inside, "There's tithe in the checkbook." She went back through to see if we had missed a week somewhere several times, but of course we had not missed. This went on for about five months until we got to the first of the year. Michele and I always set our goals in January for the coming year. However, we knew that financially things were still not right, and after several hours of investigation we found the shortages.

Was God mad at us? Absolutely not! Was He trying to teach us a lesson, so He started breaking things and making things hard? No! Did He unleash the devil on us to teach us something? No way. He was trying to help us fix it so that the bubble could be intact again. We repented, asked God to forgive us, took communion with Him, wrote the check for the difference that was missing, and made things right. I don't remember how long it was thereafter, but things stopped breaking, and they started working again. Sales started to pour back in, and life was good again. The bubble closed back up and was back in full force.

As I was very close to completing this book, I had another incident happen to me that put the KOGOS bubble on center stage in my life. It was so dramatic that this incident is the reason I wrote this chapter and drew the pictures so people can understand how the KOGOS bubble works. In 2012, I was working for this start-up company and doing extremely well. Every quarter I was exceeding my quota by significant amounts. As a matter of fact, in the first quarter of 2012, I had just come off closing the largest deal in the company's history up to that point. I brought in a new customer, which was a bank in Boston. The deal was worth just under eight hundred thousand dollars, and it put me at 200 percent of my quota for the quarter.

In May of the following quarter I went to a trade show in Boston. The first draft of this book had already been written, and God was expanding my understanding of many of the concepts in this book. At the end of the tradeshow I had to take a very short bus ride to where the parking lot was, and as I was leaving the bus I saw an iPod on the bus by my feet. There was nobody else on the bus but the bus driver. I picked up the iPod, and I don't know why, but I had the thought that nobody would claim this anyway, so I simply walked out with it.

Still to this day, I don't know why I did that. I have been extremely careful over the years to not open a door when it comes to money. As a sales rep it is very easy to add some extra mileage here and there for reimbursement. I have never done that because I knew I was operating in the blessing, and those actions would be a blessing blocker in my life.

This iPod incident happened to me in mid May (the middle of my quarter). Over the next six weeks on my job things started to get funky. I did close some business, but not much at all. As a matter of fact, we booked some deals on some very loose contingencies that ended up not coming through. Up until this point, I had always exceeded my quarterly sales quotas, but this was the first quarter in almost two years that things were very shaky. I could feel the anxiousness and pressure start to climb up on me. Although I was believing God, I knew something was not right. During this two-month window we had all kinds of things go wrong and break for us:

- The pool filter cracked and needed replacing
- The pool liner had several small tears and needed to be fixed
- The vacuum broke and stopped working
- My brand-new Jeep got dinged by a grocery cart in the parking lot
- The hot water tank broke and needed to be replaced
- We got into a dispute with our neighbor over the property line
- The lawn tractor died
- And on my job, my second-quarter sales were less than spectacular and my third-quarter sales were looking even worse

During this time I had been talking to Michele, trying to figure out what was wrong. I kind of spoke to the Lord but did not slow down much to really inquire. After two months of this I got serious about inquiring with the Lord, and the Lord answered me just like that. He told me it was the iPod. When I realized what had opened the door to my bubble, I immediately told Michele. Michele was upset with me the day I walked in with it and wanted it out of the house that day. I heard her, but I did not take action at that time.

I immediately grabbed the iPod and repented to the Lord for taking something that was not mine. I asked for His forgiveness, received His forgiveness, and then immediately drove down to Boston and brought the iPod back to the management company that would have been responsible for keeping it. Needless to say, I was pretty upset with myself because I knew much better.

Next I began to inquire of the Lord how I could get this bubble sealed back up in my life. Two nights later while at a church service, the Spirit of God came all over me, and I felt in my spirit that His anointing to prosper me was back intact in my life. The Lord then instructed me to take His

Word out and to reestablish things financially by declaring His promises for financial blessing in our lives. The very next morning I got into a place of worship and asked the Holy Spirit to lead me in how to do this, and of course, He did. He showed me what scriptures to speak, and I declared them over our lives.

At this point I thought everything was going to be grand. And although I took care of things spiritually and naturally, we were still having some residual things happening, little things still breaking. My job was better, but we weren't back to 100 percent yet. Some of the deals that I thought were going to come in got delayed and pushed out. I continued to inquire of the Lord to show me what was going on. I mean, I really prayed and asked God to reveal these things to me.

I had just written the chapter on taking your spoil, and while the other deals I thought were going to close did not, I latched on to one deal with my faith and would not let go. This deal kind of came out of nowhere, and we were in a big time competitive battle against a three-letter company that was the incumbent and known for being a sales machine. It was the last week of the quarter, and we had won it and lost it three times.

At that point in the quarter, I only had $8,000 in sales for the quarter. For a quota of $450,000, that's virtually nothing. On the very last day of the quarter, at 3:30 P.M., we were awarded the business, and I closed a deal for $725,000! This was not only a huge deal for me, but for the company as well. The company had a revenue target of $7.5 million and was only at $6.5 million until this deal came in. A little bit more business followed, and we hit our $7.5 million goal. The following week there was an article in *Forbes* magazine about how our company had become the fastest-growing data storage company of all time.

What many would call a miracle, I call putting KOGOS to work. Brother Bill Winston refers to it as "working the system." For a long time I never really understood what he meant by that, but now I do. We need to understand and work KOGOS. As we do, we will totally dominate anyone using WOS. I came to the realization that if I am in the right place with the Lord and everything is good (tithing, walking in love, etc.) then I don't need to pray and ask the Lord for anything. I simply need to take the authority that He already gave me and use it, which is what I did. I claimed that business, I bound the enemy from interfering, and I sent my angels in to bring it to me—and they did. This *is* the system that God set up, and this *is* how KOGOS works.

What did I learn about the KOGOS bubble? I learned this: God is not punishing you for screwing up. God loves you, and He wants the best for you. There are plenty that aren't living for Him and could care less about Him. So for the ones that are trying to live for Him, He's going to do everything He can to help those people live a successful life. He knows you aren't perfect, and that's not the point. You have a heart that loves Him and wants to serve Him, so He's going to move heaven and earth for people that are moving in His direction. If you're reading this book, you are one of those.

I learned this: even if you're a beginner at this KOGOS thing, whether you realize it or not, you are operating in a much more powerful system. KOGOS beginners can totally outperform the best WOS users. Read it for yourself:

> Because the foolishness of God [KOGOS] is wiser than men [WOS]; and the weakness of God [KOGOS] is stronger than men [WOS].
>
> —1 Corinthians 1:25

I also learned this: the KOGOS bubble is impenetrable from the outside. The enemy can scratch at the door and say things to you, but *only you* can open the door from the inside and give Him access into your life. Ephesians 4:27 says, "Neither give place to the devil." If the Bible says for you to not give him place, that must mean that you are in charge of it, not him.

All these principles considered, I believe that the KOGOS bubble works something like an observatory tower. I know that there are many kinds, so let me offer you a picture so we are on the same page.

When someone wants to observe the sky, the observatory doors slowly open on both sides, and when completely open, the telescope may be used. I want you to think about the KOGOS bubble working this way. I am not saying this is a "thus saith the Lord," but I personally believe this is how it works based on what I have read in the Word and based on my close observations. You'll have to go to the Lord with it.

You cannot open the KOGOS bubble from the outside, but you can open it from the inside. How does one do this? When we sin. Sin is an "inside job" after all. When you mess up, do the doors just fling wide open, completely exposing you to the curse? No. I believe Scripture teaches us that there is a grace period, giving you an opportunity to make it right before the doors begin to open. After all, God is for you; He's not against you. You're on His team, a part of His family. He's trying to help you. Make it right with Him quickly and keep your bubble intact!

How long is this grace period? I personally believe it varies based on where you are at with the Lord. We are responsible to walk in the light we have. If we walk in a lot of light, then we know better and need to fix it quickly. If we only walk in a little bit of light, then we probably have more time to come to the realization that what we did or didn't do was wrong and need to correct it. God loves you so much and wants you to enjoy the life He has for you. (See John 10:10.) He will work with you right where you are at.

If you do not rectify with the Lord within your window, then sin will begin the process of slowly opening up the KOGOS bubble. Why slowly? Again, because of God's extreme love for you! When you begin to see little traces of the curse show up, it should be a clue to you that your bubble is cracked open and to rectify it. I've always heard it said that when you make a mistake, repent quickly. Now I understand why.

First John 1:9 says, "If we confess our sins, he is faithful and just to forgive us our sins, and to cleanse us from all unrighteousness."

When you sin, your bubble opens up a crack. The longer you wait to repent, the more the bubble slowly opens up. The more the bubble opens, the more exposed you are to the curse, giving the curse greater access to your life. The curse will cause things to start breaking, will expose you to sickness, and the thief will begin to steal from you. Don't let him! Just repent quickly, and that will begin closing the doors shut. Give no place to the devil to begin to move in.

Remember, there are three governing laws to KOGOS:

- Walk in love

- Believe God

- Be led by His Spirit

Focus your life in these three areas, and the rest will follow. When you screw up, deal with it immediately. Then go to the Word in that area and build yourself up stronger. If you continue to falter in an area, ask the Holy Spirit to show you what scriptures you need to go deep in until you have a strong revelation of it. If you're not sure how to hear from the Holy Spirit yet, then use a concordance on the topic you need help with and study three to six scriptures. Get it deep in your spirit, which will make you stronger than the temptation.

Have you ever met Christians that love the Lord but just seem to live with a black cloud over their lives? You talk to them, and there's always something bad happening in their life? Sure you have. Many of them sit in church next to us. Maybe you are one of them. Let me explain what's going on. It's not that you don't have a KOGOS bubble, because every believer does. However, somewhere along the line you opened the door through sin, disobedience, not walking in love, slandering your pastor, not tithing, etc. You get the picture. You opened the door, and you never repented and made it right. Therefore, the bubble doors continue to slowly open, and if you don't make it right, it will open to the point that you are fully exposed to the curse. Although you have a bubble, your observatory doors are wide open, and the curse is having a field day because of the access you have given it.

If this is your life today, what should you do? I personally would go to the Lord and ask Him to show you where you missed it. There may be more than one area, so stay long enough until you hear from Him. Once you *know*, then you need to repent and ask Him for forgiveness. Once you have made it right with your Father, you may need to do some natural things to make it right with others. Ask the Holy Spirit about it; He will show you. Finally, I would go to the Word in that area and build yourself up so that you are stronger than whatever it was that exposed your life to the curse. This will cause your KOGOS bubble doors to seal your life up again, no longer being exposed to the curse.

How do you get stronger? I am a big fan of staying on one topic for a while and going deep, rather than just jumping from scripture to scripture

and getting surface-level knowledge. If you struggle in an area, it's per-
fectly fine to stay on one, two, or three scriptures for one, two, or three
months. This is where you work with the Holy Spirit and ask Him to reveal
it to you. The benefits are enormous!

Why do I use the example of the observatory doors to explain the
KOGOS bubble? When I picked up the iPod and walked off, it was May
15, 2012. Although I saw things getting weird around me, it wasn't until
August 9, 2012, when I took the time to hear from the Lord and repented.
On that same day I brought the iPod back. The time span on that was
about two months and three weeks.

Once I took care of everything and got the green light from the Lord
that everything was rectified and back in place, I fully expected the blessing
to turn everything around on a dime. But that is not what happened with
me. I knew I was in good standing with the Lord, but little things were
still happening. It wasn't until October 11, 2012, that we were given free
drinks at a coffee shop and my son was given a free Gatorade some place
else. You may be scratching your head wondering, what is significant about
that? However, that was the first time in over four months that we had
received something good. I believe that's the day that the KOGOS bubble
doors became fully closed again. Things stopped breaking, and the following month I closed that big deal, in November, 2012.

Please keep in mind that this happened while I was in the process of
writing the final two chapters of this book. I was constantly bringing this
to the Lord and asking Him to reveal this to me. From the time that I took
the iPod to the time that I repented and rectified things was two months
and three weeks. From the time I rectified things to the time I noticed the
blessing back in operation was two months and two days. The KOGOS
bubble seemed to open and close at about the same speed, with the closing
part seemingly going a little faster. As I brought this to the Lord, that's
where I was given the concept of the KOGOS bubble functioning similarly
to that of observatory doors opening and closing.

The purpose of my telling you this story is to provide some context
around how the KOGOS bubble operates. If you've had your doors open
for years because you didn't know any better, you do not have to wait for
years to have them close and seal your life. Remember, God is working
with you, not against you. Remember what James 4:8 says: "Draw nigh to
God, and he will draw nigh to you." You move toward Him, and that will
activate your KOGOS doors to close and seal you off from the curse.

This is a depiction of a Christian in their KOGOS bubble with the doors wide open to the curse:

This is a depiction of a Christian in their KOGOS bubble with the doors sealed, enjoying the blessing of the Lord to advance and the protection of the Lord to defend what has been given to him:

You *can* live this way. Focus on mastering the three governing laws of KOGOS and ask the Lord what you need to adjust and make it right. You can live in the very best of what the Word of God promises us. Malachi 3:10 says that as you bring your tithe, the Lord will "open the windows of heaven" over your life. Many of our church leaders refer to this as living before an open heaven.

When a believer lives in line with KOGOS, which includes bringing their tithe, I believe this is a depiction of what it looks like in the spirit realm. The Lord showed me this picture while worshipping in church one Sunday morning:

We have discussed the blessing and closing the door to the curse. Now, let's talk about what to do when your KOGOS bubble is sealed and yet you still get attacked by the enemy. You may be in the center of the will of God, but sometimes the enemy will try and put obstructions and resistance in your path to try and stop you. First, let's look at the following scriptures:

> Submit yourselves therefore to God. Resist the devil, and he will flee from you.
>
> —James 4:7

> Put on the whole armor of God, that ye may be able to stand against the wiles [devices] of the devil.... Above all, taking the shield of faith, wherewith ye shall be able to quench all the fiery darts of the wicked. And take the helmet of salvation, and the sword of the Spirit, which is the Word of God.
>
> —Ephesians 6:11, 16–17

This book was about 95 percent complete and we decided to take a family vacation down to Florida. While in Florida we made some decisions about our finances. I'm not sure if that triggered the following chain of events, but that is certainly when it started.

Three days after making these financial decisions, I was hit with a stomach bug and fell sick. We had to delay our trip, rebook our flights, and file a claim to recoup the additional tickets. A week later Michele was hit with the same stomach bug, and our toilet overflowed for hours because of it. We experienced serious water damage in our home, causing us to file a homeowner's claim. The insurance company did not want to pay us what the damage was worth and dug their heels in. I asked the Lord about it, and I received clearance from Him to hire an attorney.

While dealing with this whirlwind at home, customer opportunities were also starting to dry up. I could sense something wasn't right, but every time I went to the Lord and asked Him if I had opened the door the devil, I knew all was well with the Lord. I was not exposed anywhere.

So what was going on? I was being attacked. I did not open the door anywhere, but the enemy was obstructing my path and trying to disrupt and stop the plan of God in my life.

Shortly after coming back from Florida, I saw a fox in the back part of my woods. I remember thinking that it was pretty to look at, and I really didn't think too much about it. I have known for years that foxes are a representation of the enemy trying to steal from you. Song of Solomon 2:15 says, "Take up the foxes, the little foxes, that spoil the vines; for our vines have tender grapes."

During a three month period of knowing something wasn't right, I found myself going back to my manuscript of this book, thinking through this chapter and praying. I inquired of the Lord, and He led me to read a few pages in Rev. Nancy Dufresne's book *Causes*, and it became very clear to me what was happening to me at this time and what I was missing in this book. I had received the revelation of the KOGOS blessing bubble but had not addressed being in the will of God and just flat out getting attacked by the enemy.

During Sunday morning service the Lord showed me what I had to do and gave me the scriptures to go to battle with. He reminded me of 1 Timothy 6:12 to "fight the good fight of faith." I knew it was time to fight with the Word of God, which is the sword of the Spirit.

Early the next morning, I went into my living room, which overlooks the back woods. I have made it a discipline in my life to come into the presence of God before doing anything else. I worshipped Him, enjoyed

His presence for a while, and then I was prompted by the Holy Spirit to take the scriptures He had given to me and to go to battle. I took these scriptures and declared them and spoke directly to the enemy. Here are the scriptures the Lord gave me:

- 1 Samuel 17:43–51
- Ephesians 6:10–18
- Luke 10:19
- John 14:12
- Ephesians 1:20–23, 2:6
- Philippians 4:13
- Mark 9:23

I just followed the leading of the Holy Spirit as I declared them, resisted the enemy, and commanded him to flee. This went on for maybe twenty to thirty minutes until I knew in my heart that I had the victory. I had total peace and clearance in my heart and knew I took care of things.

My Bible was not even closed, and as I looked outside I saw some movement in the back woods. What was it? It was the fox leaving my yard! I hadn't seen him for three months. I knew the battle was won, and then all of a sudden the fox (that I did not know was there) ran out of my yard. I asked the Lord about the fox, and this is what He said to me:

> What you just saw was a natural representation of what just happened spiritually.

Wow.

I wasn't done yet though. I than reestablished what was mine by declaring the Word of God. I then instructed the angels to bring it to me. The flight insurance claim was reimbursed, sales on my job started flowing again, and the insurance company significantly increased their offer in our favor and settled out of court.

If you're in the center of the will of God and you get attacked, don't roll over. Get your instructions from the Holy Spirit and charge with the Word of God.

How do you handle an attack?

- Check first to see if your KOGOS door is open. If not, ask the Holy Spirit to lead you into this fight and battle. Don't do this on your own. Get the *rhema* Word of God on it. Do what the Holy Spirit shows you with the Word He gives you.

- Resist the enemy, take your authority, and run the enemy off.

- Once you know you have the victory, reestablish the Word of God and dispatch your angels to bring it to you.

Remember, when you're dealing with the curse, close your door, repent, make it right, and continue on in the blessing bubble.

When you're confronting an attack, get your instructions from the Holy Ghost, take the *rhema* Word, and cut his head off. Never show mercy to the enemy.

Chapter Nineteen

BLESS THOSE, CURSE THOSE

And I will bless them that bless thee, and
curse him that curseth thee.
—Genesis 12:3

I CANNOT BEGIN TO tell you how many times this particular Word has come to pass in my life. In my career there have been several times when people have come after my reputation. You know how it is in the world: people are trying to get ahead, and as such they trash talk and put down those they are in competition with to make themselves look better. And in the world system, this method works well. They target you by spreading rumors and lies, by casting doubt, and by using underhanded techniques.

This methodology of advancement works well when a WOS user is applying this curse on another WOS user's life. However, when they apply this same approach to someone living in the KOGOS bubble, something very different happens.

I worked for my last employer for twelve years. During that time I was promoted several times into higher positions of leadership. As you can imagine, there were some people that were jealous and tried to apply politics against me. The Word of God says, "I will bless those that bless thee, I will curse those that curse thee" (author's paraphrase). When I came under political attack, what would I do?

1. I would go to the Word and take authority over the spiritual attack.

2. I would declare Genesis 12:3.

3. I would pray for the salvation of God to come to that person.

If things are not right naturally, there's something going on spiritually that you need to address. Take authority, declare the Word, and pray for the person. Why would I pray for them? First, to keep my heart right so as to not short-circuit the blessing on my life. Secondly, this person doesn't know any better and is being influenced and needs salvation.

During my tenure at this company, a handful of individuals came against me over a twelve-year period. One time, a peer of mine that was a manager had been trash talking me to upper management. I did steps one, two, and three several times over a six-month period. That manager eventually got moved out of my division and moved into a different division with no influence into the management team above me.

Another time, my immediate boss was literally bullying me. He was not just being a tough manager; he was trying to hurt my reputation by using deceptive methods and making things difficult for me. Again, this was not an easy time for me, and I did steps one, two, and three for almost a year. My boss, who was a vice president, was eventually let go by the company. In both cases, they were moved out, and I stayed in the place that God had called me to and prospered.

We have had similar things happen to us with our kids' sports teams and jealous parents. We take authority over things spiritually, we declare the Word, and we pray for them and walk in love with them. We never pray for God to curse them! God does not curse anyone. God is all good and is love; therefore, how can cursing come from love?

I knew this scripture was true because it's in the Word of God. I also experienced it first had numerous times. However, I also knew that cursing does not come from God. In my quest to understand how this worked, I began inquiring of the Lord about it. A few weeks later while talking to Michele about it, the Lord revealed to me how this scripture works.

There is no defense against the curse for those in the world, regardless of who administers the curse. However, for those of us that choose to keep our KOGOS bubble closed and intact, there is a force field around us! God does not curse anyone. What the Lord Jehovah did was to set up an operating system that works the following way:

When someone is administering the curse toward you, the curse hits your force field, bounces off, and returns to jump back on the person administering it. When someone administers the blessing, it is received, and the blessing is returned to the one administering the blessing.

In the WOS system, there is no defense for the curse, and there is no blessing for advancement. In the KOGOS system, blessings are received and returned; curses are rejected and returned. God set up an operating system, and that's how it works.

Psalm 105:15 says, "Touch not mine anointed and do my prophets no harm." In the Old Testament, the anointed people were only the kings, priests, and prophets. In the new covenant, all those that call on the name of Jesus are anointed. If we'll give no place to the devil and keep our bubble sealed, then God's system will take care of the rest.

KOGOS BLESSING BUBBLE

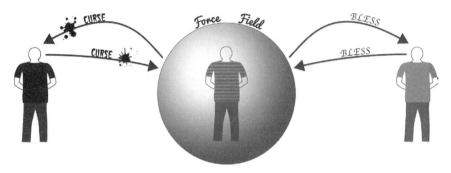

Chapter Twenty

REPROGRAM TO DEPROGRAM

O NE DAY DURING a Sunday morning worship service the Lord flashed an image in my spirit. What I saw were figures of men standing in front of me with different sized blocks and boxes in and on their head. Some of the blocks and boxes were small, some medium, and some larger. In an instant I saw the image and knew what it meant. (We call it spiritual downloads when you know a ton of information all at once.) As I drew out what I saw on my notebook, I knew the image had a double meaning.

The image I drew is nothing spectacular, but the meaning of it is very profound. Here is the image:

The first meaning was for the guys at the bottom of the picture. These are people that have mental boxes in their minds. These *mental boxes* represent the *limitations* that people put on themselves because of *their own* thinking. Although Jesus became their Savior, their own personal thinking or image about who they were and what they could and could not do limited them. Basically, their own thinking limited what they could see by faith, and therefore they never got beyond their box. Even though the Lord's resources are unlimited, these people became very limited and boxed-in by their thinking. Bill Winston refers to this as the fences in our mind. These are mental boundaries or fences that have been put up in our mind.

The second meaning had to do with the guys at the top of the picture. These are people that have with mental blocks, not boxes. In additional to boxed-in thinking, people can also have mental blocks in their minds. *Mental blocks* are *deeper-rooted* thought processes that stop people from advancing in an area. The Bible refers to them as strongholds in the mind. This is not just a fence. This is a *barricade* that has been built up with larger objects to prevent the individual from ever even thinking about passing them.

The differences are subtle yet very important. Overcoming or moving a fence is different than overcoming or moving a barricade.

But Jesus has given us the power to *expand the box* and to *remove the blocks*. When an individual becomes saved, their spirit is created in the image of Christ. This individual begins to serve a God who is limitless in power, in love, in protection, and in resources. Although their spirit becomes alive to God, 99.9 percent of their thinking remains the same. The issue is that they have been programmed to think a certain way about themselves and about how things are around them. Their programming of what they could and could not do started at an early age. Other than natural safety things, many of the limitations of the parents were passed on to the child. Over the years there were people and influences all around them that tried to program their thinking and put them in a box. Due to this programming and how they responded to this programming, some of those areas went on to become mental blocks or strongholds in the mind.

Regardless of your past, God made a way for you to reprogram your thinking to grab hold of your present and future and live life to its fullest! As a follower in Christ, you need to reprogram in order to de-program. As you reprogram your thinking in the Word of God, "right thinking" will overwrite the old piece of software in your brain. The Scriptures call it meditating on the Word. We can find this in Romans 12:2, which says, "And be not conformed to this world: but be ye transformed by the renewing of your mind." As you continue to grow in your knowledge of the Scriptures, you begin to realize who *you* are in Christ, that not only are you a son or a daughter of the Most High, but you have been made a king and a priest in the earth. You have been given all authority in the earth to rule and reign and have dominion. You begin to realize that not only does Christ own everything, but you co-own it with Him.

The majority of people who are reading this book are already Christians and more than likely walking in some measure of this faith walk. So what's the problem? Why aren't more people enjoying the fullness of Christian living? I see many Christians around me that love God with their whole heart, but they seem stuck in certain areas and seem to have reached as far as they can in those areas. Many of them may have tried to some degree for a period of time, but they kept hitting their head against the ceiling; therefore, they have plateaued. They quote Scripture with excitement but unfortunately walk in very little of it.

Remember, I am not putting anyone down here, but in order to change you have to come to terms with where you are at in your life. In the business world we call them having a "come to Jesus meeting." That's where you say it the way it is and you are confronted with one of two things: you either change or you leave. I believe you picked up this book because you want to change and grow and experience everything that God has in store for you.

Meditation in the Word is the answer to both boxes and blocks. However, the amount of labor in the Word is different for boxes (fences) than it is for blocks (barricades). You can pick up a fencepost and move it with some work. However, to remove a barricade will take more deliberate, focused, and committed work on your part. But don't worry. The work is worth it!

I have been aware of boxes or fences for most of my Christian walk. I have been meditating on the Word in many different areas and have expanded my mental boundaries significantly over the years. However, this whole notion of mental blocks took more time to identify and remove. I have had many mental blocks in my life. They have been thought processes and ideologies that had become deeply ingrained in me, so deeply that I really was not even aware of them.

The first mental block that I had to remove and overcome was in my marriage. I did not even realize I had them, but I seemed to keep stumbling over and over again in certain areas. After several years of being married, my wonderful wife, who absolutely loves me, began to recognize a common theme in certain areas of my life. Although it was difficult as a man to acknowledge them (because the need for respect is so high in a man), I knew my wife loved me, and I loved her. I chose my marriage, and I humbled myself and went to the Lord with what she was saying to me.

Once I identified that I had a mental block, what did I do? I sat down with a notepad and began to think through and write out who I wanted to be and how I wanted to act in this area. However, I wrote it in the present tense. I did not write out things that started with "I will" and "I want to." I wrote out statements about myself that started with "I am" and "I do."

I first began to write out statements like, "I am a loving husband and think about the needs of my wife before my own," and "I am a loving father and am patient with my children." I would think through this mental block in my life, which was selfishness, and write out who I wanted to be, but in the now. I would read these statements, speak them, and meditate on them until I became what I had written. The first time I did this, I can honestly say it was a process that happened over about a two-year period. I can still hear Rev. Creflo Dollar's voice in my head saying, "I'm working on something!" I was digging out a mental block in my life.

Once I recognized the first mental block in my life and realized how to remove it, it became easier the next time I came across another mental block. What was my next block? Well, whenever something new came along and I could not figure it out immediately, I would literally drop it where it was and not ever go back. One-fourth of you reading this book are thinking, "That's ridiculous! Why would you do that?" And because of your natural wiring, a.k.a. your personality trait, it's a non-issue for you. You are probably an engineer, an attorney, or an accountant.

If you can remember from my earlier description of myself, I was the guy that liked shiny new toys and would be interested in something for about five minutes. Suffice it to say, I had a mental block. What was it? My mental block was that if I could not *quickly* figure something out, then I had decided I could not figure it out at all and therefore could not do it. Obviously there were incomplete things in my house and in my life.

Eventually I realized what I was doing and asked myself, What is the root problem here? I went to the Word of God, which said I have the mind of Christ and that I can do all things through Christ which strengthens me (1 Cor 2:16; Phil. 4:13). I then went to my notepad and wrote out statements about how I could figure out anything with the help of the Holy Spirit. Thank God I did that with the help of the Holy Spirit, because I had dominoes in my future that I would have been barricaded from and would not have been able to walk in, had I not removed these mental blocks.

Your believing is specifically tied to your thinking. Your thinking is specifically tied to how you see yourself. You can read the *Logos* Word of God and even declare it, but if you haven't taken the time to meditate on it and refresh the image of how you see yourself on the inside to be in line with how God sees you, then you will simply stay as you are. You can have everything that you see in the Word! Make a decision to live a life where you are constantly growing and maturing. You will be so glad you did!

Chapter Twenty-One

THINK BIGGER

ROVERBS 23:7 SAYS, "As he [a man] thinketh in his heart, so is he." I don't care how you slice and dice it; *how you think* is directly tied to your *faith*. And your faith is directly tied to how you think. If the Scriptures say all things are possible to them who believe, then there are no limitations with your faith. The boundaries that you are continually pushing out are the boundaries of your thought process. As a man or woman of God, there are no actual limitations to you. The only limitations are those perceived or fabricated limitations in your thinking.

Before you got saved there were real limitations in your life. It was based on who you were, who you knew, where you came from, and how much money you had. Now none of that matters. You are in the family of the Kingdom of God, and if you use KOGOS those old rules and limitations no longer apply to you. There's a whole set of new policies that apply to you, and literally the sky's the limit.

Here's my point: regardless of how you think that you think, you are thinking too small! The purpose of this chapter is to expand your thinking, knock down the fences, and blow up the box that limits your thinking! I thoroughly expect this section to challenge your thinking as it relates to finances. At least that's the goal.

I'm going to use a section from Rick Renner's book, *Sparkling Gems* to lay the foundation and push the boundaries of your thinking. Page 130 is titled "Filthy Stinking Rich" and begins with 1 Corinthians 1:5–6, which says:

> In every thing ye are enriched by Him, in all utterance, and in all knowledge, even as the testimony of Christ was confirmed in you.

The word *rich* means to have goods, property, and money in abundance; to have possession of abundant resource, material goods, and significant wealth; to have more than enough to gratify one's normal needs or

desires. Rev. Renner begins this section by describing the word *enriched* in
1 Corinthians 1:5–6:

> The word "enriched" is the Greek word *plousios*, which describes
> *extreme or vast material wealth*. In fact, the word *plousios* is
> where we get the term "plutocrat," referring to a person who is
> so prosperous that he is unable to ascertain the full extent of
> his own wealth. Because of his investments, his companies, and
> the percentage of interest he earns on his portfolio all grow so
> rapidly, it is impossible for his accountants and bookkeepers to
> keep track of how much wealth he actually possess.
>
> Can you imagine being so rich that no one can figure out
> how much you own or control? Well, that is the description of
> a *"plutocrat"*!
>
> Now Paul uses this same word plousios in First Corinthians
> 1:5 when he says we are "enriched by Him..." The Greek word
> for "by" in this verse is the word *en*: and in this verse, it can
> be translated either *in Him* or *by Him*. This conveys two very
> powerful truths to you and me:
>
> The day we were born again and placed *into Jesus Christ* was
> the richest day of our lives. On that day, we literally become
> *joint heirs* with Jesus Christ, with a legal right to all the prom-
> ises of God! Indeed, that was a rich day for all of us! In light
> of this, First Corinthians 1:5 could be interpreted, "...*We were
> made rich the day we were placed into Him...*"
>
> But the Greek word en could also emphasize the point that
> just as we were enriched the day we got saved, this enrichment
> process continues throughout our lives as we walk with God.
> The verse could thus be interpreted, "...*We are continually
> being enriched as a result of being in Him...*"
>
> Because the word *plousios* is used, this verse conveys the fol-
> lowing idea:
>
> "...*You are invested with great spiritual riches because you
> are in Him, and that's not all! The longer you remain in Him,
> you just keep getting blessed with more and more wealth that
> comes from being in Him.*"[1]

Rev. Renner goes on to talk about how the apostle Paul was actually referring to spiritual riches when he wrote to the Corinthian church. As the Corinthian church continued in Jesus, the gifts of the Spirit grew stronger and as such, they were made spiritually richer. Rev. Renner concludes this section by advising us not to settle for spiritual poverty because we are now *spiritual plutocrats*, loaded with spiritual gifts and treasures.

When I first read this chapter by Rick Renner, the words *can you imagine* jumped off the page at me. I knew the Holy Spirit was instructing me to use the imagination that God had given me and to allow the Holy Spirit to paint the image of a plutocrat in my spirit. It was almost as if the Holy Spirit were asking me, "Steve, can you imagine it? Do you dare to allow yourself to go there and see your self that way?" And I said, "Yes, I will imagine it." (By the way, I am still working on this.)

So here is what I wrote on the pages of this chapter:

> Imagine myself so rich from my numerous companies, investments, and interest I earn from my vast amount of wealth that numerous accountants that work for me can't keep track of how much I own and possess because it just grows too quickly.
>
> Imagine it. Meditate [on] it. Allow the Holy Spirit to paint the picture, the image, the living movie on my heart, in my spirit. I am a joint heir in Christ and with Christ. Jesus is the richest; there is no one richer. He is my business partner. Everything He owns, I own.
>
> Richer then Bill Gates, Steve Jobs and Warren Buffet put together. A *plutocrat* of *plutocrats*.

Now, what am I doing by writing this out and reading it and meditating on it often? I am expanding my thinking and pushing those fences way, way, way out. The key is not whether I have this yet or not. When I wrote this, I had owned no companies and had no investments to speak of. But what I am doing is sharing with you the process the Holy Spirit brings me through to expand my thinking, which expands my faith containers. The Scriptures tell us that as a man thinks in his heart, so is he. *Your thinking will take you somewhere.* When you work with the Holy Spirit in this manner, He will begin to move you in that direction. It all begins with how you think.

So I ask you, Can you imagine it? If you have never done this before, you probably just choked on what you just read. I have been working on this for a while. But you can begin with wherever you are at right now.

Ask yourself this question: What would it be like to make three times what I am currently making? Now for most of you, your mind will immediately say, "How could that ever happen? There's just no way." That's just your mental box or fence that's trying to limit your thinking. Tell it to shut up. Now, let's start again. This time *allow your mind to go there,* and allow yourself to *actually think about what life would be like* earning three times what you are earning today. Tell your mind to be quiet, and just do it. There's some work involved to knock down a fence. This is what you are currently doing.

How does your life change? Think about it. How would you live differently? Imagine it. How much pressure would that take off of you? Where would you live? Where would you vacation? What would that allow you to do? What would that allow you to give? Now take the time to stay here and think this through. Allow the Holy Spirit to paint this image in your spirit.

Have you ever walked into a store and seen the sign that says, "Your husband called and said you can buy anything you want"? Well, I'm here to tell you that your "husband," Jesus (your provider, your caretaker) wrote you a letter and told you, you can live any way you want. The sky's the limit. Take the time to meditate on the Word, and use your God-given imagination and allow the Holy Spirit to expand your thinking, which expands your faith containers. Instead of always getting thirty-, sixty-, and one-hundred-fold full all of Dixie cups, you can begin to enjoy thirty-, sixty-, and one-hundred-fold full of buckets, barrels, dump trucks, and beyond.

But that's just it. There are no limitations in Him. It's up to you and what you can believe. As long as it's based on the Word of God, then you're good to go. The work you have to do is meditating the Word of God. Once you see it, then asked the Holy Spirit what corresponding action you can put forth that lines up with what you are believing. When you get to this point, declaring the Word of God is a piece of cake.

No matter how big you *think* you're thinking, *think bigger.*

Chapter Twenty-Two

STOREHOUSES AND THE PIE

OVER THE YEARS, Michele and I have grown in our relationship and understanding of the Lord. But like anything, if you are not careful it's easy to allow other people's ideas to seep into your thinking and get you out of balance. You may be pretty good in most areas, yet get a little off in another area, and it causes you to be out of balance. Have you ever heard a washing machine that spins out of balance? Most of the machine is working just fine, but because it's out of balance it makes a pretty loud noise.

Michele and I have been tithers and givers since we first got married. As the years went on we began to grow in our revelation in understanding for God's plan to financially prosper His people. We listened, we studied, we read and meditated, and God continued to reveal layers of revelation to us. I'm not sure where, but somewhere along the line we developed an all-or-nothing attitude. If you have ever studied personality traits and have heard the term Type A, then you know these people are driven people. Michele and I both score fairly high in this area. So I think part of our issue was the way we were naturally wired to be results-driven people, and I think the other contributing factor consisted of comments that had been made from full-time priests as to what they would do if and when they came into money.

We found ourselves in a thought process that was almost negotiating with the Lord, making statements like, "Lord, bring us millions of dollars, and we will put it all into the gospel." Although that sounds right, it has a thought process that is out of balance. It is very subtle and seems right, but it is out of balance, like a washing machine can get out of balance.

When you first read this, you might think I'm crazy or even think I am contradicting myself. Let me clarify one thing: it is absolutely right to have a heart that is willing to give it all. I believe the Lord can absolutely use a heart that is soft, open, and willing. But a thought process that believes that you are expected to give it all or give till it hurts is simply out of balance.

You may hear well-meaning Christians or even ministers that reference the story of the woman that gave her last two mites and use that scripture to say that you must give it all for the Lord. To come away with that understanding would be to take that verse of scripture in a vacuum. Generally speaking, the Scriptures do not teach that. I do believe that there are times that the Lord may ask us to give it all, but I believe it needs to be Holy Spirit initiated. And if the Holy Spirit initiates it, it's because there is a bigger plan behind it that you do not see. In this case, your obedience and faith in this area will walk you into the next domino of provision.

This is what I believe happened to the woman with the two mites. I believe this woman was praying and asking the Lord for help because she had very little. I believe the Lord prompted her to give her two mites. Jesus saw it and commented on it. Now, the Scriptures do not say much after that regarding the woman, but having had this situation happen to me, and knowing the Lord, I have a really good idea what happened to this woman. God brought increase into her life that sustained her through this difficult time.

When Michele and I were married for about five years, we owned a duplex, we just had a baby, and we made the decision that Michele would stay home with our children. In the business world that means that our revenues dropped and our cost structure went up! At about that time my sales job went from a salary-plus-commission job to a straight commission job. If you don't sell, you don't get paid anything.

Each month we seemed to be a little short, and were taking out two hundred to three hundred dollars a month just to pay our bills and make ends meet. We didn't have a lot in our savings, maybe twenty-five hundred or so. Michele prayed about it and asked the Lord what the deal was, and He said, "That's what it's there for," referring to our savings account. That wasn't the answer we were looking for. We didn't totally understand the answer at the time. But He's the Lord, and we trusted Him, so we were OK with what He said to us.

After about six months, we found our savings had dwindled down to about one thousand dollars. That's not much. I was becoming discontent with my job, and I had prayed about it and felt like it was time to make a change. I left the industry I was in and went into a brand-new industry I knew nothing about, telecommunications. We had been praying about this change, and I felt it was right in my heart, so I went with the company I had a peace about.

In the meantime, it bears mentioning that Michele was a saver; I was not. My philosophy was, if we had it, let's go spend it! Needless to say, we were getting stressed at home about our financial situation. We prayed to the Lord about our financial situation and asked Him to help us.

There was a guest minister at our church for the week, and we went to several of the services. One night while sitting near the front, the Lord spoke very clearly to me and told me to write a seven hundred dollar offering. I heard Him so clearly, and His presence was strong on me to do it. As I sat there and began to think about it and talk to Michele, I could feel the cold sweat coming down my forehead. *What?* That was almost everything we had left! We would virtually have no cushion, and the thought of it was scary to me. I had a decision to make while sitting in that seat. Was I going to trust the Lord? Or, was I going to do what I thought was best and go based on what I knew and saw in the natural? What would you do?

Michele and I talked as we sat there, and we knew that we needed to obey the Lord in this. Although we didn't understand it or see how things were going to go for us, we knew that He loved us, and we trusted Him. So we took out our checkbook and wrote an offering for seven hundred dollars, and we did it in faith. We laid hands on it and spoke the Word of God to it and believed Him for the return.

I'm thinking something like this happened to the woman with the two mites. The Scriptures do not describe anything of what happened before she gave the offering or after she gave the offering—just that she gave all that she had. God's not a thief. He is God, Jehovah the Good! All goodness comes from Him. He is love, all love, and the best that there is comes from Him and to those that trust Him.

I had just started my new job...and during first month on the job I earned a commission check of seven thousand dollars. *Yes!* That was on top of a pretty good salary! In one month we had gone from three hundred dollars in the savings to having several thousand dollars back in there. In this situation, a seven-hundred-dollar seed prompted by the Holy Spirit became a seven-thousand-dollar harvest.

What do you think happened to the woman? This is what I believe happened. She prayed and asked the Lord for help. Some time later He prompted her to give the two mites. Jesus saw it and commented on it in the Scriptures. From there, I absolutely believe that a large chunk of money found its way to her. There's no way that didn't happen!

As for me, I doubled my income that year. The following year I made even more, and at the age of thirty I made a six-figure income for the first time ever. In two years' time I went from barely making ends meet, using the savings that we had to sustain us for some time, and believing God to help us to being prompted to give a very large amount and receiving a tenfold return in one month and doubling our income.

Are there times God specifically tells you to give all? Yes, He does. However, do not get out of balance to think that He's always telling you to do that. When the Lord speaks, you do it; it's just that simple. If He doesn't tell you to give it all, then you live your life within the guidelines of the Scriptures.

I believe the Scriptures provide a balance in the way we handle our finances. Generally speaking, it's not all or nothing. I believe there are four primary areas that have to do with money.

1. Tithe (Mal. 3:10)

2. Offerings (2 Cor. 9:6–11)

3. Storehouses (Deut. 28:8)

4. Living (Matt. 6:31–33)

The tithe is a clear-cut thing. The tithe is 10 percent of all increase that comes into your hands. There is no praying or seeking God as it relates to the tithe because the Scriptures are very clear that 10% of all increase belongs to the Lord. You have entered into a covenant of exchange with the Lord. You bring the tithe in faith to Him, and He brings the blessing, which brings increase into your life (Proverbs 10:22). He puts His power on you, which acts like a magnet and draws increase to you. The tithe is the starting point for operating in the Kingdom of God.

The next three areas are where people can get out of balance. This is where we were out of balance. We knew things were not quite right in our thinking in regard to the way we were managing and handling our finances. The Lord started speaking to Michele regarding storehouses. She kept coming to me and telling me the Lord was speaking to her strongly about having storehouses in our life, so we went back to the Word and inquired more about it with the Lord. We had a savings account or two, but we were not using them as a tool for increase.

Let me explain what I mean. Basically, the Lord first reemphasized that storehouses are scriptural and right. The Lord spoke to Joseph and urged him to build storehouses. If Joseph had not obeyed, a lot of people would have died that were not supposed to. Even during our season where what was coming in was not enough to pay the bills, the Lord said that our savings account (our storehouse) was there and available for that reason.

But now the Lord began showing us how to use the combination of storehouses and our faith together as a tool to cause increase to come to us. He showed us to set up different savings accounts for the different things we are believing for. The first principle here is that this is *corresponding action to our faith*. In other words, this is something that we can do that lines up with our faith. The second principle is that now the *money has a specific place to go*. The money we were believing God for in these different areas now had a home or a target to land in.

We saw it! So we put into action what God showed us and began to ask ourselves, what are the different things we are currently believing God for? We set up different savings accounts according to our faith. We set up savings accounts for things such as college tuition for each kid, vehicles, vacations, and several other things that we were believing God for at the time. All I can say is what happened next was amazing. Money began to find its way into these different savings accounts.

The analogy that God showed us was that when we tithe, the Lord causes the rain to come down on us. In this example the rain is increase that He is pouring out on us (Mal. 3:10–11). However, previously we had no place for the rain to go, so the rain ran down the hill and seeped back into the ground. When God showed us to set up different savings accounts according to our faith we began putting buckets on the ground for the rain to go into. Each bucket had a name on it. They were the names of each savings account. We put faith buckets in our life, and they began to get filled up. You can call them faith buckets or faith containers; they mean the same thing.

Michele and I were blown away at what was happening in our savings accounts. Shortly thereafter, we were listening to a teaching series by Rev. Bill Winston. During one of his teachings he made the statement, "Sow some, save some, and spend some." Because we had already been meditating and seeking the Lord, we were able to hear when the rest of the revelation came. What he said came alive in our hearts.

I titled this chapter "Storehouses and the Pie" for this reason. God spoke to us about storehouses to give money a place to go. God spoke to us through Rev. Winston about how to manage our money as a pie. There are multiple slices in a pie, just like there are multiple places the Lord would have you put your money. Every time money comes in to us, it gets divided into multiple slices. The slices are not all the same size and can vary in their size from time to time. You will have to inquire of the Lord and ask Him to show you how He would have you handle your finances in this area.

You need to bring your tithe in faith, and then you "sow some, save some, and spend some" with the rest of your finances. Your finances have four places to go, and the Holy Spirit will guide you and instruct you on how much goes where.

1. Tithe (10 percent)

2. Sow some

3. Save some

4. Spend some

As we have moved through this journey, every time we meditated on something on purpose, we begin to see things we didn't see before. Do you remember those paintings that came out in the nineties? After you would stare at them for a period of time your eyes would eventually come out of focus, and you would see an image of something beautiful that previously you did not see. This is how meditating on the Word works to change your perception. Once you get hold of the Word, now you see something different, and your reality has now changed. Although the natural—the picture of what it looks like when you first look at it—has not changed, you see a new reality for your life.

Once that happens you begin to make different decisions based on your new reality of what you see. From there, it's as if you've tapped into another world or dimension that others don't see, but it's massively real to you. You begin to recognize things that God has prepared for you that previously did not seem to be there. You recognize answers (wisdom downloads) and resources that God has brought to you. All of this has continually happened to us every time we meditate on something on purpose. In the example above we were seeking the Lord and meditating and were then able to *recognize* when our answer came to us. We simply did what God showed us to do, and our finances totally changed for the good.

Let me show you why that is. Jeremiah 17:5–8 is quoted below, but I'm going to break it down in a different way for you to see it:

WOS:

> Thus saith the LORD; Cursed be the man that *trusteth in man*, and maketh flesh his arm, and whose heart departed from the LORD. For he shall be like the heath in the desert, and *shall not see when good cometh*; but shall inherit the parched places in the wilderness, in a salt land and not inhabited.
>
> —JEREMIAH 17:5–6, EMPHASIS ADDED

This man was a believer but chose not to follow the Lord. This man chose to use WOS to make decisions for his life. Again, I want you to think about your laptop or computer. Whatever operating system you choose to use, you are limited to or bound by the governing laws or rules of that operating system. The man in the scripture above chose WOS to live his life by.

In this operating system there are no applications that allow him to see or recognize "good." There is no access to this other realm or dimension where "good," answers, or resources from the Lord come from. It simply just does not exist in WOS. There are no applications to access this type of data in this operating system.

Another analogy would be to say that the Web sites where all of this great information and rich media exists have been blocked to the users of this operating system. They cannot get access to it; they can't even see it and don't know that it exists. That is why this man "shall not see when good cometh" and this man lives in "the parched places in the wilderness."

Let's look at the next verse:

KOGOS:

> Blessed is the man that *trusteth in the* LORD, and whose hope the Lord is. For he shall be as a tree planted by the waters, and that spreadeth out her roots by the river, and *shall not see when the heat cometh*, but her leaf shall be green; and shall not be careful in the year of drought, neither shall cease from yielding fruit.
>
> —JEREMIAH 17:7–8, EMPHASIS ADDED

This second man made the decision to trust in the Lord and chose to use KOGOS. By choosing this operating system to live his life by, he has access to and lives in a totally different dimension or reality. He has access to data, rich media, revelation, resources, and wisdom downloads that do not even exist to those that choose WOS. These two men could both be sitting in a coffee shop, both of them sipping a cup of coffee, and both have their laptops in front of them. Yet, they live in two totally different dimensions and reality.

The first man cannot recognize, see, or access the dimension of "good," because to that man it does not exist. The second man lives in the dimension of "good," and to that man "parched places in the wilderness" do not exist. He cannot see it or access it in the KOGOS. Those Web sites that have malicious code, malware, and computer bugs cannot access him. This man only sees good.

For many Christians, although they have one laptop, they move in and out of two different operating systems in their lives. If that's you, you need to recognize this and make a decision which operating system you are going to live your life by.

James 1:8 says, "A double minded man is unstable in all his ways." This was me until I got a revelation of these principles. I was using KOGOS 80 percent of the time for my life, and then for the other 20 percent that had to do with my finances I was using WOS. Is there any wonder why I was not living in the fullness of what the Scriptures said I already had? I was frustrated that I was only living in a small portion of what I knew God had already provided for me. Once I realized what I had been doing I decommissioned the old operating system and fully cut over to using the KOGOS 100 percent of the time.

For many believers, they move in and out of KOGOS and WOS. This is the reason they feel like they are running in the mud and never getting very far. When we fully cut over to KOGOS, life began to change dramatically for us. We took a sledge-hammer to that old, familiar operating system and destroyed it. More importantly, we have developed a lifestyle of using one operating system forever, and that is KOGOS. We have moved into heaven on earth, which was God's plan all along for all of us. You will need to come to the same decision as well. Go KOGOS all the way! It's now your time.

Chapter Twenty-Three

PUTTING ON THE MIND OF CHRIST

IN THIS BOOK, we have been highlighting the differences between KOGOS and WOS. WOS is filled with limitations, shortcomings, and is riddled with malware and bugs. KOGOS, however, was created by the Master Developer Himself, God the Father. His OS is perfect, and for the user it has unlimited potential. The Master Developer created His OS in order for the user to experience the same results as if the Master Developer gave the commands Himself. As a matter of fact, when the user follows KOGOS and issues commands, KOGOS doesn't know the difference! It is a perfect system that works every time when it's worked properly by the user.

In KOGOS, there is an additional component that the user has available to them that's not available in WOS. It's called the mind of Christ. In 1 Corinthians 2:16 it says, "We have the mind of Christ." In Philippians 2:5 it says, "Let this mind be in you, which was also in Christ Jesus." I know the Word says, "Let this mind be in you." However, I want to change the wording to help you understand the analogy. In Ephesians 6:11 it tells us to "put on the whole armour of God." I want to use the same wording as it relates to the mind of Christ.

I was meditating on these things one day and the words "put on the mind of Christ" came up in my spirit with a picture. I'm not a big gamer. However, I saw the picture of a gamer's virtual headpiece with the words *mind of Christ* across the top. The picture I saw looked like this:

MIND OF CHRIST

I immediately drew the picture and wrote out the words that I saw. I thought about how a gamer would put on his virtual headpiece, and as he did so he would enter into another virtual reality or dimension. He could see things and experience things that no one else around him had access to or even knew existed. When a gamer puts on his headpiece he enters into a whole knew dimension that did not exist without the headpiece. He transforms himself from just an average Joe to a giant in this game. In real life, the gamer may not be very impressive in terms of what he can do naturally speaking. However, when he puts this headpiece on he can see things that no one else can see. He can do things that naturally speaking, he cannot do. In this new dimension, he has abilities, resources, and weaponry that he did not have sitting on the couch.

As I continued to think about this picture the Lord gave me, I also began to think about actual military soldiers and how our military needed to make improvements in their ability to accomplish tasks at night; thus, nighttime vision equipment was created. Without nighttime vision equipment, a soldier is very limited in what he can accomplish in the dark. If he can only see a few feet with his natural sight, he will not be able to accomplish much. However, a soldier that is equipped with nighttime vision equipment can now see what he could not see previously. If there are two military forces in the same woods at night, and one of them has nighttime vision equipment and the other does not it is very obvious who will come out victorious.

When you let this mind be in you, or as I like to say, "put on the mind of Christ," it's like putting on your gamer headpiece and putting on your nighttime vision equipment. You enter a dimension that others do not realize exists. You can see what others cannot see. Because your vision has dramatically improved, how you think changes to be in line with this other dimension. In this dimension, you can do what you could not do before. You have access to resources and weaponry that didn't even exist until you put on the mind of Christ headpiece.

You can be a Christian and not put on the mind of Christ. As a matter of fact, many Christians live their whole lives without putting on the mind of Christ. Even though their spirit was created in the image of God, they still think the old way, the natural way, man's way, with all of its limitations and lower-level thinking. Even though as a Christian you have access to a whole other dimension and realm, when you *don't* put on the mind of Christ you are reduced to minimal seeing, minimal thinking, and minimal resources. The person living this way is a Christian who loves God but is actually using WOS in their thinking and how they live.

When you put on the Mind of Christ, you can see what nobody else can see. You can think in a manner that others do not have access to. You can be in command and in authority in matters concerning your life, and unlimited resources become instantly available to you because you chose to operate or live your life according to KOGOS.

Isaiah 55:8–11 illustrates this truth. In the Old Testament, the mind of Christ from KOGOS was not even an option. The anointing of God was only available to the king, the priest, and the prophet. The anointing was not available to the masses. The power of the Holy Spirit would come on these three offices, but the Holy Spirit did not take up residency in His people until after Jesus paid the price and God the Father sent the Holy Spirit to live inside of us. Therefore in the Old Testament, everyone's thoughts were natural, worldly, limited, and radically reduced. That's why Isaiah 55:1 says, "Your thoughts are not my thoughts, and your ways are not my ways" (author's paraphrase), and that His thoughts are "higher," or another way to describe that would be that His thoughts (thinking, seeing, resources, etc.) are in another dimension or realm (KOGOS). Higher-level thinking or being was not even possible for the masses of people in the Old Testament.

But now it is! Once you accept Jesus as your Savior and are filled with the Spirit of God, you become a candidate to live according to KOGOS. How do you put on the mind of Christ? By meditating on His Word and allowing the Holy Spirit to bring you into this other dimension. (We in the Christian circles call this revelation from the Word of God.) You can now begin to see what He sees and think what He thinks.

As a Christian, you have a choice. You can either walk around in the dark, doing it man's way, or you can choose to put on the KOGOS equipment that God has given to you. When you put on the mind of Christ, you can see what nobody else can see and think on a level that is not even available to the masses of unsaved and the saved that still use WOS.

Let's once again take Elisha as an example. In 2 Kings 6 we read that the city that Elisha was staying in was surrounded by the king of Syria's army with "horses, and chariots, and a great host" (v. 14). When Elisha's servant saw this, he panicked. But Elisha did not panic, because Elisha was using KOGOS and saw into another dimension that nobody else could see. In 2 Kings 6:16–17, Elisha says, "And he answered, Fear not: for they that be with us are more than they that be with them. And Elisha prayed, and said,

LORD, I pray thee, open his eyes, that he may see. And the LORD opened the eyes of the young man; and he saw: and, behold, the mountain was full of horses and chariots of fire round about Elisha."

The Lord wants you to put on the mind of Christ so that you can see the reality of the Kingdom of God. Why is this so important? Because what you see effects how you think, which effects the decisions that you make.

Seeing -------------- → Thinking -------------------- → Decisions

The servant only had natural, limited sight. He was using WOS. Elisha was using KOGOS and could see what nobody else could see. He could see the Kingdom of God because he was using the Kingdom of God operating system. The servant saw no way out; therefore, he was probably thinking of turning himself in, which he would have done if it were not for Elisha.

Elisha, on the other hand, saw another reality, which caused his thought process to be very different (higher) than the servant, and he therefore made a very different decision. He used KOGOS to issue a command (v. 18) and led that army to the king of Israel.

Why does the phrase "put on the mind of Christ as a headpiece" make sense to me? Because it reminds me that as a Christian I have two operating systems that I can choose to live by. One moment I can be using KOGOS, and if I'm not careful the next day I could be using WOS. The system I use determines what I see, which determines how I think, which determines the decisions I make. It helps remind me to make sure I am seeing my life and the decisions that are before me through KOGOS.

The reality is, as Christians we all have the mind of Christ! There is nothing to "put on" like some spiritual headpiece; it's already in you! Meditate on the promises of God and allow the Holy Spirit to reveal it to you. The purpose of this chapter and analogy is to make you aware that there is another reality in KOGOS and for you to develop a lifestyle of thinking and operating according to KOGOS. Remember, if you can see it in KOGOS, you can have it.

What decisions are currently in front of you that you've realized you have only been seeing and thinking about on the lower level (WOS)?

Think about Elisha's situation again.

The only reason Elisha was surrounded by the Syrian army was because Elisha was spiritually hearing their plans miles away. That is impossible using WOS, but normal when using KOGOS. Was Elisha concerned when the army showed up? No. Why? Because Elisha could see into the realm of the spirit that the Lord's army was present. That is impossible using WOS, but normal when using KOGOS.

When the servant came out, he could only see with his natural sight. Therefore, he was petrified. How these two individuals considered handling the situation was *very different* based on what they saw.

Naturally speaking, they were both looking at the same problem, but one of them was using KOGOS, and the other was using WOS. It wasn't until Elisha prayed and asked the Lord to let him see according to KOGOS that the servant began to breathe deeply because *he knew* it was going to be all right. How could he be so sure? Because he shifted from using WOS to using KOGOS, and his entire perspective changed. The reality was, his answer—God's protection in this case—was there all along, but he couldn't see it until he began to use KOGOS.

What system are you using right now? Do you use WOS the majority of the time without even realizing it? What you see affects your decisions. What decisions are you currently facing where you are not seeing what God has already done for you because you have not been operating with the mind of Christ? God has already provided everything you could ever need, and it's sitting there in the realm of the spirit waiting for you to call upon it.

Although KOGOS was not available to everyone in the Old Testament, it is absolutely available and has been paid for you to operate in the New Testament. KOGOS is for every believer; as a matter of fact, it is the very reason Jesus came to the earth. He came to reestablish His Kingdom, which is putting us back in charge of the earth, just like Adam was before he fell.

Let's take this subject into the New Testament since this is where we live today, and let me walk you through this process in the same manner the Lord walked me through it.

Often I will ask the Lord for a scripture to stand on for my job. During one sales quarter I asked the Lord for a scripture to stand on, and He gave me Romans 8:28, which says, "And we know that all things work together for good to them that love God, to them who are the called according to his purpose." I meditated on this scripture for months, and the Lord began to reveal it to me in a picture. "All things work together for good"—God has dominoes of good already preplanned and prearranged for you to walk in. Understanding that they are preplanned from before you were born allows the couple of words before it to be true. It begins with "for we know," which means "to intimately know or to be fully persuaded of this truth." When can you be fully persuaded that all things work together for good? When you are in line with the rest of the verse, which are your two guardrails:

1. "Love God": Walk in love

2. "Called according to His purpose": Follow His plan for your life

When you are living your life according to these two simple guardrails, they will keep you in the center of the will of God for your life, and you'll walk right into dominoes of Good.

Please just take a moment right now and think about *how much* God loves you. He planned your *entire life* out and put an amazing arrangement of good things throughout your future!

A few months later I was praying in the spirit one morning, and the Lord led me to read Philippians 4:13 out loud: "I can do all things through Christ which strengtheneth me." Notice the verse does not say *who* strengthens, but it says *which* strengthens me. This scripture is actually referring to the anointing or the power of the Holy Spirit. In that sense, Philippians 4:13 could also be read this way: "I can do all things through the power of the Holy Spirit, which gives me the strength or the power to accomplish it."

When I read Philippians 4:13 out loud, the words "all things" jumped off the page. Where had I read that before? Romans 8:28 says, "All things work together for good." Therefore, there are three things that work together. They are:

1. "Love God": Walk in love

2. "According to His purpose": Follow His plan for your life

3. By the leading and power of the Holy Spirit

If you think about these two verses together, they are saying the following:

For we know and are fully persuaded that you can do all things that will turn out for your good (because God Himself set dominoes of good things in your life) when you are walking in love, when you follow His plan, and when you allow the Holy Spirit to lead you to them. When the Holy Spirit leads you to them, His power (His anointing) is present in and on you to bring that thing to pass for your good.

Please take some time to process this picture; it is the culmination of all these things we just reviewed:

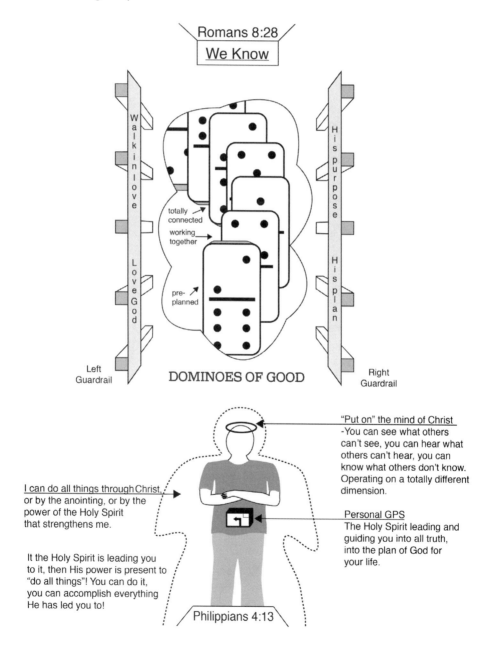

KOGOS power *always* overrides WOS power and all natural laws. You see, non-covenant people use WOS power, which is very limited and doesn't always work. WOS is a broken system and is subject to all natural laws. That is the reason the scripture says:

Matthew 19:26: "With men it is impossible; but with God all things are possible".

In the context of this book, this scripture could also be read this way:

> With men that use WOS it is impossible due to the limitations
> of their natural ability and the limitations of natural laws, but
> when you use KOGOS, all things are possible to you. There are
> no limitations to a believer that uses KOGOS.

Remember, we started this chapter on the mind of Christ. I was talking to Michele one morning about this topic and about my ability to get results on my job, and she looked at me and told me that my gifting was following the Holy Spirit. If you thought about this comment naturally speaking, you might want to get offended and insulted. Was I insulted? Not at all! Here's what she was saying: "Steve, when you follow the leading of the Holy Spirit, you far surpass anything the super intellectuals can do." Wow.

Now I say this to you: When you follow the leading of the Holy Spirit (use KOGOS, not WOS), you can far surpass anything the super intellectuals can do. It's almost not even fair! But it is, because we know God and they don't. Why would you try and beat them at their own game? Their game is WOS. Why would you try and outperform them using their system? Change the game on them! If you are a believer who has a job, you can *see, hear, know,* and *perform* on a level that the unsaved don't even have access to!

The mind of Christ is *not* superior natural thinking. Some may be tempted to think that the mind of Christ is something like Albert Einstein's mind but maybe ten times greater. That maybe it's something like a super intellectual's mind but multiplied to a higher level. But that's not it at all. A gifted, super intellectual mind is on a totally lower level and is absolutely inferior to the mind of Christ. The mind of Christ is far, far, far beyond what the smartest, most gifted intellectuals could ever achieve. These people are the smartest people on the lowest level mind, the natural mind. The mind of Christ is not natural thinking at all; it is spiritual thinking. It is seeing, knowing, hearing, and performing by the Spirit of God.

In 1 Corinthians 2:14, Paul talks about how God's ways "are foolishness unto him [the natural man]." The reality is that the world operates on a much lower level, and they just can't comprehend KOGOS. It is just way beyond them. It makes no sense to them; they can't understand it, and they can't decode it. It is like gibberish or foolishness to them. It's like an infant trying to understand calculus. It's just way beyond their comprehension.

KOGOS is a system and a government that's on a level that non-believers don't even have access to.

- KOGOS provides spiritual seeing that natural sight cannot see.

- KOGOS provides spiritual hearing that natural hearing cannot hear.

- KOGOS provides spiritual knowing that the natural mind and natural thinking cannot know.

- KOGOS provides spiritual power to accomplish results that natural ability cannot accomplish.

KOGOS operates on a totally different realm that natural men using WOS have no access to. Read Isaiah 55:8–9 and 1 Corinthians 2:6–16 and ask the Holy Spirit to reveal it to you.

WOS may or may not bring natural answers to your situation now, but KOGOS will bring the wisdom of God now. WOS may or may not bring finances to your situation over time, but KOGOS will bring finances now. WOS may or may not bring healing to your situation over time, but KOGOS will bring healing now.

If you have come to the realization that you have been using WOS, don't get discouraged. Instead, thank Him that He showed it to you! Why? Because now you can begin your journey using KOGOS and walk in the fullness of what God has planned for you from before the foundation of the earth!

Chapter Twenty-Four

IN IT, NOT OF IT

THERE HAVE BEEN many misconceptions and myths in the church as it relates to money, business, the world, and Christians. I have heard all kinds of things said by Christians and even some ministers in these areas that just are not right. For a long time many in the church believed that poverty was some type of badge of humility. The enemy was able to infiltrate the ranks with this method, and as a result the church body had very little financial resources to get things done.

Obviously this is not what the Scriptures teach. The Lord began to speak to many of his leaders in the body and began to clarify the big difference between money and greed. Greed is evil. Money, however, is a tool, and a very important one at that. As time went on, we gave this philosophy a name and called it the prosperity message. The Scriptures are very clear: if you think poor, you will be poor. If you are poor, there is no extra to help build churches, youth centers, outreaches, to make a mortgage payment for someone, or buy a single mother groceries for a month.

First Timothy 6:17–18 says, "Charge them that are rich in this world, that they be not highminded, *nor trust* in uncertain riches, but in the living *God, who giveth us richly all things to enjoy*; That they do good, that they be rich in good works, *ready to distribute, willing to communicate.*" Scripture says to not put your trust in riches. It does not say to not have riches. Quite the opposite, He wants to richly give you all things to enjoy!

If you are a parent, don't you enjoy giving your kids nice things? I sure do. It makes me happy, especially when they are grateful to me and know that I'm doing it because I love that. Wow, there's nothing better than that. God is totally excited when your heart is close to Him. As you use your faith to believe Him, He is able to pour out richly all things to you, and *out of your abundance* you are able to distribute it and establish the Kingdom of God in the earth.

I've heard it said that God is extravagant but never wasteful. Remember, God owns it all. There is no shortage of anything with the Lord. He is unlimited in His resources.

If your mentality is "just enough for us, Lord, and no more," you may think you're being humble, but I would tell you, you are being selfish. Michele and I had a friend many years ago that could no longer afford her apartment, and so we invited her to live with us for a month or two to help her get established. While she was staying with us she made the statement to me with a big, humble smile that all she really wanted was a couch to sleep on. This was someone that had a great heart for people, was very involved in ministry, and very giving of her time. She was a wonderful person that loved the Lord and people. When she made that statement to me I looked at her square in the eyes and said to her, "You selfish thing." She looked at me with shock and horror on her face. It was as if I had just slapped her across the face, and she could not believe what she had just heard. Obviously, this was the complete opposite of what she thought she was actually doing.

I went on to explain to her two things. First of all, if all she ever wants is a couch to sleep on, that would be all she would ever have. The Lord will give her exactly what she believes—"According to your faith be it unto you" (Matt. 9:29). Secondly, although her thought process sounded like a good Christian idea, it was actually selfish because all she was thinking about was herself. She absolutely gave no thought to helping other people or ministries *financially* because she didn't have any extra to give. She gave plenty of her time, because she had that, but very little money because she did not have much to give. She had little because she believed for little.

Let me tell you something: God is not going to override your will or what you believe. If you believe Him for a couch, He has plenty of them in the Kingdom of God. If you believe Him for a beautiful home on the water with a pile of extra money in excess of what you need, He has plenty of that in the Kingdom of God too. He has plenty of teaspoons and plenty of dump trucks in the Kingdom. The Lord has plenty of both, and it all belongs to Him *and* you together. If you are a tither, the Lord will pour it out on you. How much you keep in your life is based on your faith container. Teaspoons, buckets, dump trucks, or warehouses—you determine it. Here's what I am saying. If you will begin to believe Him for much more than just for you and yours, you can begin to participate in establishing His Kingdom financially in the earth.

Another misconception that exists in the body of Christ is the manner in which they work for the money or receive the money. This misguided thought process shows up in many different ways with many different variations. It's the thought process that says, "We are to have nothing to do with the world." The thought process then continues to believe that what they do for a job should be as minimal as possible so that they can limit their interaction with the world.

Many of these Christians think that if they pursue advancement in their jobs somehow they are becoming more like the world, and they don't want to do that. Many of them think that all types of investments are bad, and why should they bother anyway because that's what the world does. "They go after money, and I don't want to be like the world."

The result is, the Christians that believe this line of thinking end up having very little resources to get things done. Let's say, for example, that the pastor wants to buy a bus to pick up people in the inner city and bring them to church. If you are one of these people, you might be able to squeeze out twenty or fifty dollars toward this. Here's the only problem. There are hundreds of people, and you need several buses. It may take several years to buy what's needed to help these people. But what if you could write a check for one thousand, five thousand, or even twenty thousand dollars and it not impact your daily living one bit? Is it wrong to have extra money beyond your needs? Or are you now able to help establish His Kingdom in the earth?

Another thing that happens is that they weaken their influence into the lives of nonbelievers. You've heard it said, "Money makes the world go round." In their system, (nonbelievers that operate in WOS) they are right. They get to build homes, buy cars, take vacations, put their kids into good schools, provide for their families, and so on. If you don't have much money or have less than the non-believers you interact with, much of what you say to them will often get minimized or disqualified. They may not tell you they are doing this, but most of them are.

Why? Because in their system, *money* is both a *god* and a *tool.* They worship money. Money is *the* most important thing. Money is number one. As a result, their lives are built upon getting more of it. If you have more of it, you rise in influence in their eyes. They want to know how you got it. They become more interested and are attracted by it. If you have less of it, you have less influence in their lives. If they are much better off financially than you are, what you say has less credibility in their minds. Don't get mad at me for stating the facts. This is how it is in WOS.

Let's think about this for a moment, though. Doesn't it take money to do those things for us too? Don't we need money to build homes, provide for our families, and so on? Yes. Therefore, money is what is used in our system too. What's the difference? There are two distinct differences that I see. First, to them money is their god. They serve it. To us, the Lord Jesus is our God. We serve Him! With them, they will do whatever it takes to get it. With us, we access it by our faith. Do you see the difference?

However, in both systems money is the means of exchange. In a sense it makes the world go round, but in our system, money is just a tool, though it is important because according to the Scripture in Deuteronomy 8:18, we *need* money to establish His Kingdom. For Christians, it's a question of *how* we get it, *not if* we have it. The question that follows that, then, is: Are we following the Lord's system or man's system to get it? We need money, and lots of it! However, in our system it's already been provided for. Romans 8:32 says, "He that spared not his own Son, but delivered him up for us all, how shall he not with him also *freely* give us *all things*?" (emphasis added).

A Christian's desire not to be of the world is right, but for many Christians the application of being in it but not of it has been wrong. In other words, your heart is right for wanting to obey the Lord and follow the Scriptures, but how you're applying them in this example is incorrect. Joseph was in the world but not of it. His heart was for the Lord, and He was following the Lord's system, KOGOS. The Lord eventually placed him to be the number two boss running the world's economy. Joseph was placed smack dab in the center of the world's economy. Do you realize that?

We as Christians are in the earth. We run big corporations, we are in government, we are professional athletes, we are leaders, builders, inventors, investors, and so on. The difference is the operating system we use! Are we using KOGOS or WOS? Joseph followed the Lord and did what the Lord told him to do. He was using KOGOS. The question is not *if* we are in the earth; that question is, *How* are we functioning in the earth? Are we using the world's system to function or the Kingdom of God's system to function?

First John 2:15 says, "Love not the world, neither the things that are in the world." The next verse describes what he means: lust of the flesh, lust of the eyes, and pride. In other words: selfishness, greed and arrogance. We should be fully functioning in the earth but not operate like they do. This is a very important point. *All* money and *all* financial resources in the earth belong to the Lord and to His people. Vast amounts of money do not belong to non-believers, although many of them possess it. If money and getting the money is wrong, dirty, and bad, why would the Lord be giving you power to get more of it? If you think that limiting your job and thus limiting your income results in not being of the world, then why is the Lord giving you power to get more money? Can you see how the application of this scripture is incorrect?

The Scriptures say to be in the world but not of it. This has nothing to do with getting money, advancing in your career, building a successful business, or making investments. Being in the world but not of it to me has to do with what operating system you are using while you are doing what you are doing.

Everyone is born into the earth. The decisions that you make determine the operating system that you follow, not how much money you make from your job or business. I'm going to use the analogy I used earlier in the book to help make this crystal clear.

Let's assume that everyone is born with a laptop in their hands. If you are given a laptop, you are expected to use it. You will learn how to hit the keys to create words and sentences. You'll learn how to use the mouse to click on things of interest and so on. The question here is not whether or not you should be using your laptop. The question or the issue here is, What operating system are you using in your laptop? Are you using the WOS or are you using the KOGOS? Being in the earth and functioning in the earth, such as working and making money, are equivalent to having a laptop and learning how to use it. If the Lord gives you a laptop, He expects you to use it. Well, the Lord put you in the earth; He expects you to use the resources that He put in the earth for you.

There are three types of people as I see it, and how you answer the following question determines who you are. The question you need to answer is, What system are you using while you're functioning in the earth?

1. Are you keeping your heart close to the Lord, tithing, believing, and trusting in His plan as the Holy Spirit leads you into the next step, the next domino in your life? If so, then you are using KOGOS. You are in the world, but not of the world, and God can use you big time. You have power on you from the Holy Spirit and function in a bubble of blessing and protection. (Romans 8:14: "For as many as are led by the Spirit of God, they are the sons of God.")

2. You make all the decisions for your life. You're not entirely sure there even is a God, but if there is, you sure wish He would help you get ahead in life. What you need is more money, and that's really the problem; you don't have enough of it. If this is you, you are using the world's system to live. This is man's way, when you have your hands upon the wheel of your life and you do what you think is right. (Proverbs 14:12: "There is a way which seemeth right unto a man, but the end thereof are the ways of death.")

3. The third way is the most common for Christians and the real problem area. Do you love the Lord with your whole heart, but when it comes to making decisions you think you take the time to quickly pray about it, then make a decision and ask the Lord to bless it? You rarely slow down to ask the Holy Spirit to direct you into His plan. If you do, it's only for a brief moment before you run off in the direction you think makes the most sense to you. If so, you are flip-flopping between operating systems. Although you love the Lord, you mostly use man's ways with the request of the Lord's blessing on it. On occasion you get yourself in such a deep hole that you dust off God's ways and try to figure out how to do it right, because what you did screwed things up pretty bad. (James 1:5–8, "If any of you lack wisdom, let him ask of God, that giveth to all men liberally, and upbraideth not; and it shall be given him. But let him ask in faith [use God's system], nothing wavering. For he that wavereth [flips back and forth between operating systems] is like a wave of the sea driven with the wind and tossed. For let not that man think that he shall receive any thing of the Lord. A double minded man [a man that actively uses two operating systems] is unstable in all his ways.")

Having a job or a business and making money is like having a laptop and learning how to use it. There is absolutely nothing worldly or evil about that. The question has to do with what system are you using while functioning in the world. Are you using God's system, or are you using the world's system?

Allow me to take on one more misconception that I often hear and that has to do with working a secular job. What makes a job secular? I know traditional church definitions would say that you're a Christian with a secular job. We have defined a secular job as any job in the world, unless of course the owner is a Christian or if you work for the church, then that's not secular. It's this definition that has caused a conflict and internal struggle with many Christians.

I would define a secular job not by the job but rather by *the system* you use to perform the job. The job doesn't make it secular. What system did you use to get the job? And what system do you use to perform the job? The Lord is never going to lead you to a bad job. If you follow KOGOS to get the job and KOGOS to perform the job, then you are in the place that the Kingdom of God designed for you to be in, and that's not secular. If the Holy Spirit led you to it, then it's a KOGOS, God-designed, and God-ordained kingly function and ordination. Allow God to use you to the fullest!

Allow me to summarize what I think the Lord is saying when He says to be in the world but not of the world:

> Son or daughter, I created an amazing, spectacular, one-of-a-kind you with tremendous gifts and talents. Before you were ever born I created an amazing plan for your life, a far better plan than anything you could ever achieve or enjoy on your own. I created you to look like Me and act like Me with My love in your heart and My Spirit inside of you to help you, lead you, and guide you into My plan. I then placed you in this earth and have already orchestrated a path and a way of life for you to richly enjoy all of My creation. As a matter of fact, I have created you to be a king and a priest in your home and in every area I have called you to. I have created you to rule, to lead, and to reign in the area of domain that I have given to you.
>
> I expect you to lead with love as you follow the leading of My Spirit into the plan I have already designed for you. I have placed unlimited resources in the earth. These resources belong to Me, and as such they belong to you too. In order to fulfill My plan, you will need to follow the system that I have laid out in the Scriptures to follow. As you seek My plan and follow the leading of My Spirit, I will walk you right into people, places, and all the resources you will ever need and more, because I

am a God of abundance. I am establishing My kingdom in the earth, and you play an important role in My plan. Trust in Me, follow the system of how I operate, and you will thoroughly enjoy and fulfill the life that I created for you from before the creation of the world.

Chapter Twenty-Five

FOUR PILLARS FOR OPTIMAL PERFORMANCE

A LL OPERATING SYSTEMS are designed to work at optimal performance, and KOGOS is no different. As with any operating system, there are many things that can impact or degrade the performance. The same is true of KOGOS. Rather than focus on the things that can slow down our performance, I have decided to focus on what I call the four pillars for KOGOS optimal performance.

For all of my super technical readers, I know I have oversimplified my next explanation. However, I have chosen to keep it simple for non-technical readers to understand, as it is more important that people understand the concepts rather then putting non-technical people to sleep.

An operating system is written by developers. Developers write code that basically sets the rules and standards for how the software is going to operate. God the Father is the Master Developer that wrote KOGOS (the Kingdom of God operating system). He wants us to understand it, know it, and master it. We are His people and part of His team. He is the developer of KOGOS and made us the administrators of KOGOS.

In the IT world, an administrator is one who runs, manages, and is responsible for a particular system. If that system or application is not working well, the business calls on the administrator to look into it and figure out how to get it working at optimal performance. If it's not working at optimal performance, it can have a huge impact on the business.

In like manner, the Lord has made us the administrators of His operating system, KOGOS. He expects us to learn it, master it, and be responsible for making sure KOGOS is operating at optimal performance *in our lives*. If it's not, it's our responsibility to make sure that these four key pillars are in place to ensure optimal performance of KOGOS in our lives.

The four pillars for optimal performance in KOGOS are:

- Relational
- Locational

- Navigational

- Operational

Relational has to do with fellowship, which is absolutely the most important and the starting point for everything with KOGOS. "Relational" means that you have an intimate connection and closeness with the Lord. It means that you live your life with your heart close to and connected with Him throughout the course of the day. It means that you are in tune with Him and are very aware of His reality in your everyday life. This pillar means a lifestyle of intimacy and closeness with the Lord.

Kings need to make this a priority in their life. Because kings are called to business, they function in a performance-based environment. There is constant external pressure to perform at a high level. Kings need to keep their relationship with the Lord first, resist the external pressure, and continue to operate using KOGOS. There will be times where the pressure and the stress will try to push you. *Remember, Jesus is your secret weapon. Worldly kings have no access to Him or His power, but you do.* Stay close and connected with Him. Worship Him and inquire of Him for help, wisdom, or whatever it is you need. Jesus is your source for everything. If you are in the right location, then everything you need is already there in abundance.

Locational has to do with your calling and the plan of God for your life. Are you currently in the right location or area that God has called you to? If you are in business, did God call you to that job, business, or occupation that you are in? It is possible that you have a good relationship with the Lord but that you've made your own decision in this area and that you are in the wrong location, doing something God has not called you to do. In real estate and in business they use the phrase "location, location, location." If you are in the right location for your business, you have a far greater chance of succeeding. The same is true with the Lord. He has a specific location that He has designed and orchestrated in advance for you. If you are in the location that God has called you to, your probability for success goes up dramatically. God has people, resources, connections—everything you could ever need in the *location* He has prepared for you.

Navigational has to do with following the leading of the Holy Spirit in the day-to-day decisions for your life. Most of the kings that I have met are very driven, success-based, results-orientated individuals. Many are what we call Type A personalities. Because of that, many kings get themselves into trouble when they come to the Lord with a preset plan and ask Him to bless it. Kings want to build, succeed, and conquer. Add to that their driven nature, and they are constantly thinking of ways to do so. Rather than coming to the Lord with your own plan (which causes you to use WOS), slow down and take the time to ask Him what His plan is.

This was a big adjustment for me and probably will be for you. You have been in control of your destiny with your hands firmly gripped onto the steering wheel and your right foot pushed all the way down to the floor, going to *your* next destination as fast as you can. What I am advising you to do is to slow down and take the time to look at the navigation system that God put inside of you. Your personal GPS already has a set destination and directions on how to get there. The Holy Spirit (the Spirit of God, the Father, Himself) contains the plan of God with every microscopic detail for your life. Allow the Holy Spirit to navigate the day-to-day decisions of your life. By the way, I have never had so much fun and excitement as I do living this way. If you want a life full of adventure, live this way. There is nothing better. I challenge you! (Kings never refuse a challenge!)

Operational has to do with the way God wired you to operate. *Operate* means the way you get things done, how to execute the plan to accomplish the task. Other people may try to tell you how you should accomplish something or how you should get the job done. God has wired you and has prepared you to operate a certain way that works in conjunction with the anointing and calling for you.

Let's use King Saul and King David as an example. Both Saul and David were kings. However, Saul was appointed king out of the request of the people. God hand-picked David and anointed him to be king. Saul was a trained warrior and knew how to use the weapons from his training. David kept his heart close to Lord, stayed connected to the Lord, and God prepared him the way that God had for him. Over many years of a close heart, God prepared David a certain way that may have seemed unconventional or insignificant. In this preparation, David had to overcome the attacks of the lion and the bear. Think Karate Kid; he was prepared in an unconventional manner, yet when it was time to compete he conquered his enemy and won.

David caught wind of Goliath and went in to Saul. David said he was going to take Goliath down. Saul wanted to put *Saul's* weapons on him and tried to get David to slay the giant *Saul's way*. But that was not how God had prepared David to operate. God prepared David a different way, and when David operated in the way that God prepared him for, the anointing of God (the power of God) came upon David. When David chose to operate the way God had prepared him, the king's anointing on his life was operating at optimal performance in David's life. David could have chosen to operate Saul's way, but I'm not sure he would have had the same outcome.

God has wired you to operate a certain way. When you operate the way God has wired you, the anointing of God will be working at optimal performance in your life.

Finally, I would like to discuss the relationship between kings and priests and how they need to function together for optimal performance in the Kingdom of God. Priests are called to minister to the Lord and to minister the gospel to the people. God will give the priest the vision and the plan for the call of God on their life. Kings are called to bring the wealth in, in order to build the Kingdom of God. Kings are called to bring in the provision to accomplish the vision. Both kings and priests are anointed to fulfill the call of God on their lives. Both kings and priests are responsible for following the leading of the Holy Spirit to fulfill the call of God on their lives. Both are equally necessary and function in very different roles for the building of the Kingdom of God. Kings think about ways to get the wealth in. Priests think about ways to get the gospel out. In spite of their different functions, kings and priests are to respect each other and work together as the Holy Spirit leads them.

Let me just say one thing to the kings here. You are *not* in charge of what God has called the priest to do. God put that priest in charge of that ministry, not you. We need to respect each other's roles and learn to function together the way God created us to.

When kings and priests recognize their divine relationships and live in line with the four pillars for optimal performance—relational, locational, navigational, and operational—there is no stopping the building and establishment of the Kingdom of God in the earth!

Chapter Twenty-Six

UNDER GRACE

A s you have learned in this book, there are two operating systems that are available to believers. Even though I have laid out some concepts and high-tech analogies on how certain things work, this entire book would have missed the mark if you came away thinking that God's system is based on your performance.

KOGOS is not performance-based, it is grace based.

> For sin shall not have dominion over you: for *ye are* not under the law, but *under grace.*
>
> —ROMANS 6:14

You are under grace. Let's set the right foundation as it relates to salvation first, and then we'll talk about every other area in your life. For many of us, we have had to unlearn old thinking and relearn new thinking. Before we were saved we were under the Law, and many of us were trying to achieve righteousness by our performance and our good works. Finally there came a point in time when we realized that it didn't matter what we did; our righteousness and good works fell short, and we needed a Savior.

We had a sin nature and as a result were prisoners of sin. We were under the Law, standing upon our righteousness and building up our good works to try and make it. Yet we were under the Law, and the weight of sin and our sin nature made it impossible to connect with God.

For someone that does not know the Lord, their life spiritually looks like this:

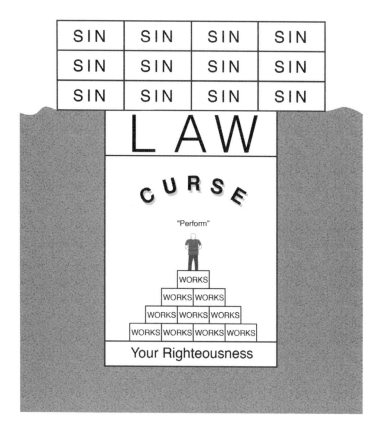

When you accepted Jesus as your Savior, you literally became a new creation on the inside.

> Therefore if any man be in Christ, he is a new creature: old things are passed away; behold, all things are become new.
> —2 CORINTHIANS 5:17

What does that mean? The great exchange happened! When you accepted Jesus, He removed you from being a prisoner of sin, and you became and took on the righteousness of God because of your faith in the blood of Jesus. Jesus destroyed that sin nature and created you to be just like Him, the righteousness of God. Through one man's disobedience, you took on your sin nature. By accepting Jesus' gift to you, you took on the *righteousness of God.* You may make a mistake and mess up, but that does not change your nature on the inside. At the very core of who you are, you are righteous. When God the Father sees you, He sees Jesus.

> Therefore by the deeds of the law there shall no flesh be justi-
> fied in his site: for by the law is the knowledge of sin. But now
> the righteousness of God without the law is manifested...Even
> the righteousness of God which is by faith of Jesus Christ unto
> all and upon all them that believe...Being justified freely by his
> grace through the redemption that is in Christ Jesus.
> —ROMANS 3:20–24

What does this have to do with using KOGOS and being under grace? Everything! WOS is based on man's performance. KOGOS is based on grace. The Kingdom of God operating system is a grace-based system, not a performance-based system. If grace is the engine that runs KOGOS, then believing in Jesus (and His Word) is the fuel that makes it go. It is not your performance that makes grace work; it is your trusting and believing in Jesus that makes grace work. That's it.

> Trust in the LORD with all thine heart; and lean not unto thine
> own understanding.
> —PROVERBS 3:5

> Therefore it is of faith [believing], that it might be by grace; to
> the end the promise might be sure to all the seed; not to that
> only which is of the law, but to that also which is of the faith of
> Abraham; who is the father of us all.
> —ROMANS 4:16

Grace is the Lord's unmerited favor. You didn't do anything to earn it, deserve it, or perform good works for it. He just gave you His favor because you believe in Him. Living under His grace provides you with total, complete, and full access to *all of His resources*. Grace gives you access and full rights to everything Jesus has access and rights to—and that's everything, my friend.

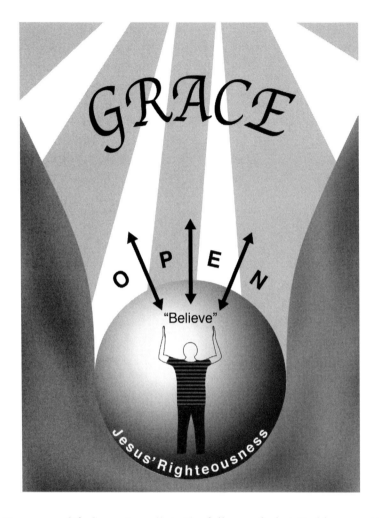

You are qualified now to walk in the fullness of what God has provided to you because of your faith in Jesus! You are under His grace; you have become the righteousness of God, and all of heaven's resources are available to you.

> For the promise, that he should be the heir of the world, was not to Abraham, or to his seed, through the law, but through the righteousness of faith.... Therefore it is of faith, that it might be by grace.
>
> —Romans 4:13, 16

Now that we have set this right in your mind, let's talk about going on the offense. Many Christians spend much of their time trying to hold on to the little bit that they have, a defensive mind-set. And although there is absolutely a place for defense, many Christians have never gone on the offense using KOGOS!

Think about this: You live under an open heaven, under grace, totally and completely righteous, an heir of salvation, an heir of the world—and you have all of heaven's resources available, standing at attention, listening earnestly for KOGOS commands to come out of your mouth.

> Herein is our love made perfect, that we may have boldness in
> the day of judgment: because *as he is, so are we in this world*.
> —1 JOHN 4:17

In the New Living Translation it says, "And as we live in God, our love grows more perfect. So we will not be afraid on the day of judgment, but we can face him with confidence because *we live like Jesus here in this world*" (emphasis added).

Romans 5:1–2 in *The Message* Bible crystallizes it for us:

> By entering through faith into what God has always wanted to
> do for us—set us right with him, make us fit for him—we have
> it all together with God because of our Master Jesus. And that's
> not all: We throw open our doors to God and discover at the
> same moment that he has already thrown open his door to us.
> We find ourselves standing where we always hoped we might
> stand—out in the wide open spaces of God's grace and glory,
> standing tall and shouting our praise.

After having read these scriptures, look at the grace picture above one more time.

KOGOS is not hard, because Jesus is not hard. Jesus is easy. Living for Jesus is easy. You can boil all of KOGOS down to three main things. If you focus the rest of your life on these three things, you will live a life that is full, you will fulfill the plan God for your life, and the Father will be well pleased with you.

KOGOS: Love. Believe. Follow.

That's it. It's just that simple. Love the Lord and love people. Trust and believe in Him. Follow what He tells you to do. It's really that simple.

What do most people do? They try to accomplish things on their own and then go to grace to fill in the gaps or mercy to keep them from falling off the cliff.

Most believers have it in this order:

1. I do everything I can.

2. I ask God for His help when I fall short.

Instead of doing what you can on your own (WOS) and then turning to God when it doesn't work, simplify your life and use KOGOS. KOGOS actually works this way:

1. Trust in and rely upon Jesus, His grace.

2. Do whatever He tells you to do.

KOGOS does not work by trying to earn it and perform it. Your job is to believe Him for the promise and then follow the Holy Spirit in what He has you to do. It is not your job to perform the healing or to create the wealth. Your job is to believe Him for the healing, believe Him for the wealth, and then do what He shows you to do to walk in it.

> Therefore it is of faith, that it might be by grace; to the end the promise might be sure to all the seed.
>
> —ROMANS 4:16

KOGOS: Love. Believe. Follow.

Chapter Twenty-Seven

MY STORY

THANK YOU FOR reading this book. I hope it has helped and continues to help you. The Lord told me to call it a handbook. I hope you refer to the pages of this book often as you grow in KOGOS. Below are some of my final thoughts on my journey thus far.

- God's power only works with *His* plan. Seek His plan and His KOGOS system, and His power to prosper you will follow.

- The Lord *led me* to the telecom company. I learned a tremendous amount and had several *seasons* of development followed by seasons of advancement.

- Ten years later the Lord *prepared me* for change—change that actually did not come until two years later (*timing*).

- The Lord then *led me* to this little start-up company with thirty-plus employees. It was a crummy office that looked like nothing at the time.

- This high-tech company was going to solve a big, complex problem with technology I didn't even understand—but I *trusted Him*. I left what was a comfortable, good-paying job to follow the promptings of the Holy Spirit into something I knew nothing about.

- There were turns in the road that I did not expect. At one point, I even thought I was going to lose my job. But through all of the turns I stayed *close and connected* to the Lord, and He kept me in the center of where He brought me.

- At times the circumstances could have caused me to make a natural decision and get out of the will of God. But instead, I would *check my spirit,* and every time it would be "clear skies and blue water." I would also *reread* the things the

Lord told me to help settle me. (I journal when the Lord speaks to me.)

- The first couple of years, I had to work extra hard in conjunction with following KOGOS. For those couple of years, working extra hard to learn things I did not know was the *corresponding action* to my faith. However, it was not my work but rather my believing and trusting in Jesus and doing the things He showed me to do that brought me the business and big commission checks. I learned to use my faith and His grace as an offensive weapon to walk in the promises of God.

- As I lived close and connected to the Lord, I would periodically *take inventory* with myself to make sure I was actually using and implementing KOGOS in my life and in my business.

At this high-tech company, I worked with some of the most talented people in the world. These people were the best and brightest in their fields and in their countries. And yet I found myself repeatedly being the number one sales person in this company.

Some might say that I had a lot of help along the way from a lot of people, and I would agree.

Some might say that my engineers played a big role in our success, and I would agree.

Some might say I had a huge advantage in being located at our headquarters and that I probably would not have been as successful if I were at a remote site, and I would agree.

Some might say that I was given a lot of extra time for others to teach me about the industry I was in and that help made a big difference, and I would agree.

Some might say that I am the luckiest guy in the world, and I just happen to time this right, and according to their WOS perspective I would agree.

But that is the whole point of seeking the plan of God and following the Lord! God knew *all* of this! He knew the incredible talent that would be there and the amazing technology that would be created, and He stuck me smack dab in the middle of it! He even put me in this company five months before the president and many other extremely talented people, which gave me the time to learn the basics of what I needed.

Remember, although this is my journey, it is certainly *not* about me. My journey, my story, and this book have everything to do with the Lord Jesus, the plan He has for you, and the grace you are under. This is about Him.

I learned a lot from my president, my manager, my engineers, and especially from my CEO—all of whom I was honored to work with and for. There were times that I had to work a little harder than others or would have to go back and fix a mistake that I had made in my sales process. Even still, you need to remember the key to this whole thing: *I was in the center of the will of God for my life, operating under His grace.* Even if I made a mistake or even if I was deficient in an area, it was still going to work out to my benefit no matter what.

The Lord Himself had led me there; therefore, I was operating in the *grace zone*. What is the grace zone? It is operating from a position of *strength*, a position of *power*, a position of *"there's no way you can fail."* It's where the Lord Himself has already lined up people, provisions, wisdom, help, finances, business, and so on *for your success.*

Where do most believers live? In the mercy zone. It's where you go off on your own and you do your own thing. You move yourself away from the power and the provision that was lined up for you, and you end up in the woods of life—and God's doing His best to keep the curse off of you.

So what was different about me as compared to probably most of the other sales people at this company? I used and trusted KOGOS, so I had *spiritual power* on me that caused things to go in my favor. They just had their natural WOS ability. KOGOS is usually not spectacular or dramatic, but it is *supernatural.* People would ask me how on earth I got some of the deals I got. The answer is, I would operate according to KOGOS and put what I had learned to work. I would issue my take your spoil commands, and then I would do what I knew to do naturally speaking as a sales person (my corresponding action). I landed some really big deals with some very large companies and seriously tough competition.

The apostle Paul used KOGOS:

> But God hath chosen the foolish things of the world to confound the wise; and God hath chosen the weak things of the world to confound the things which are mighty.
>
> —1 CORINTHIANS 1:27

Unto me, who am less than the least of all saints, is this grace given, that I should preach among the Gentiles the unsearchable riches of Christ.

—EPHESIANS 3:8

KOGOS was my secret weapon.

In Acts 10:34 it says that "God is no respecter of persons." KOGOS will work for everyone that will follow the Lord and His operating system.

KOGOS will work for you.

NOTES

CHAPTER 1: KINGS AND PRIESTS

1. Todd Burpo, *Heaven Is for Real* (Nashville, TN: Thomas Nelson, 2010), 125.

CHAPTER 7: GUARDRAILS

1. Merriam-Webster Dictionary Online, s.v. "guardrails," http://www.websters-online-dictionary.org/definition/guard+rail (accessed September 17, 2013).
2. Kenneth E. Hagin, *How You Can Be Led by the Spirit of God* (Tulsa, OK: Faith Library Publications, 1986), 11–12, 25–27, 87, 126.4.
3. Kenneth E. Hagin, *Plans, Purposes, and Pursuits* (Tulsa, OK: Faith Library Publications, 1986), 9, 29, 38–41.

CHAPTER 9: THE MOUNTAIN OF GOD

1. Kenneth Copeland, feat. Bill Winston, Believer's Voice of Victory, television broadcast, February 22–26; March 1–5, 2010.

CHAPTER 10: TIMING AND YOUR PERSONAL GPS

1. Kenneth E. Hagin, *Plans, Purposes, and Pursuits*, 38–39.
2. Rick Renner, *Sparkling Gems From the Greek* (Tulsa, OK: Harrison House, 2003), 462.

CHAPTER 12: TWO REALMS BLENDED TOGETHER

1. Wikipedia.org, s.v. "Electromagnetic spectrum," http://en.wikipedia.org/wiki/electromagnetic_spectrum#Range_of_the_spectrum (accessed September 4, 2013).

CHAPTER 15: TAKE YOUR SPOIL

1. Copeland, Believer's Voice of Victory, February 22–26; March 1–5, 2010.
2. Kenneth E. Hagin, *How God Taught Me About Prosperity* (Tulsa, OK: Kenneth Hagin Ministries, 1985).

CHAPTER 17: HOW IT WORKS

1. Gary L. Wood, *A Place Called Heaven* (Mustang, OK: Tate Publishing, 2008), 60–62.

CHAPTER 18: THE KOGOS BUBBLE

1. Nancy Dufresne, *Causes* (Murrieta, CA: Ed Dufresne Ministries, 2009), 7–9.

CHAPTER 21: THINK BIGGER

1. Renner, 130–131.

ABOUT THE AUTHOR

STEVE RICHARD HAS been led by the Lord to work for three start-up companies over his career, having held numerous positions, from sales rep to regional vice president. Most recently, he was the number one sales rep in one of the fastest-growing high-tech companies of all time. From the age of nineteen he has been a diligent student of the Word and has learned how to use God's system successfully in the competitive business world. These principles have led Steve to have a successful marriage, family life, and career in sales and sales management. Steve lives in New Hampshire with his wife, Michele, and three children.

A King's Journey begins with the story of how the Lord led Steve to work for one of the hottest high-tech start-up companies of all time. Having come from outside the high-tech industry, Steve knew nothing and had to believe God and follow the leading of the Holy Spirit as He led him from company zero to company hero. The second half of the book contains all of the principles the Lord revealed to Steve about how to be successful in the world using God's system instead of using man's system.

CONTACT THE AUTHOR

Steve Richard can be contacted at KOGOS4life@gmail.com.

ARTIST

ANDREW SPENCER IS currently a student at Cedarville University studying graphic and web design. He can be contacted at andrew.spencer.business@gmail.com.

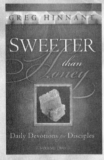